PRAYERS AND MEDITATIONS OF
THÉRÈSE OF LISIEUX

Prayers and Meditations of Thérèse of Lisieux

Edited by
Cindy Cavnar

CHARIS

Servant Publications
Ann Arbor, Michigan

Published by Servant Publications
P.O. Box 8617
Ann Arbor, Michigan 48107

The editor and the publisher wish to express their gratitude to the following for permission to reprint material.

From *The Autobiography of St. Thérèse of Lisieux* by St. Thérèse of Lisieux, translated by John Beevers, Translation copyright © 1957 by Doubleday, a division of Bantam Doubleday Dell Publishing Group, Inc. Used by permission of Doubleday, a division of Bantam Doubleday Dell Publishing Group, Inc.

From *Story of a Soul,* Translated by John Clarke, O.C.D. © 1975, 1976 by Washington Province of Discalced Carmelite Friars, Inc., ICS Publications, 2131 Lincoln Road, N.E., Washington, D.C. 20002 U.S.A.

From *General Correspondence I,* Translated by John Clarke, O.C.D. © 1982 Washington Province of Discalced Carmelite Friars, Inc. 1982, ICS Publications, 2131 Lincoln Road, N.E., Washington, D.C. 20002 U.S.A.

From *General Correspondence II,* Translated by John Clarke, O.C.D. © 1982 Washington Province of Discalced Carmelite Friars, Inc. 1988, ICS Publications, 2131 Lincoln Road, N.E., Washington, D.C. 20002 U.S.A

While every effort has been made to trace copyright holders, if there should be any error or omission, the publishers will be happy to rectify this at the first opportunity.

Cover design by Michael Andaloro

01 10 9

Printed in the United States of America

ISBN 0-89283-749-7

Library of Congress Cataloging-in-Publication Data

Thérèse de Lisieux, Saint, 1873-1897
    Prayers and meditations of Thérèse of Lisieux : edited by Cindy Cavnar.
        p.   cm.
    ISBN 0-89283-749-7
    1. Catholic Church—Prayer—books and devotions—English.   I. Cavnar, Cindy.
    II. Title.
BX2179.T49E5 1992
242-dc20
                                                                    92-38010

Contents

Note to the Reader

THE MATERIAL in the following chapters focuses on key themes in Thérèse's spirituality. It is intended for use in personal prayer and reflection. In each chapter, excerpts from her prayers and meditations follow a major theme and are interspersed with commentary that situates them in her life and spirituality. Each chapter then concludes with a reflection and a prayer.

After reading and reflecting on the prayers and meditations in a particular chapter, you may want to use the closing reflection and prayer to guide you in your own time of personal prayer. Or you may decide to linger over a prayer or meditation earlier in the chapter that seems particularly apt to your situation.

However you use this book, it is my sincere hope that these prayers and meditations will inspire you to love God with all your heart and to seek his will for your life—whatever that involves. Then you will truly be following in the footsteps of Thérèse of Lisieux and in the footsteps of Jesus.

Introduction

———◆◆———

SAINTS, ALMOST BY DEFINITION, are larger than life—at least in the popular imagination. We want our saints tough, like St. Anthony who fasted in the desert for eighty-five years. We want them brave, like St. Felicity who went to her martyrdom only hours after giving birth. We like it if they were notorious sinners prior to their conversion, like St. Camillus who drank heavily and was addicted to gambling. We're happy if they were exceptionally gentle, like St. Francis of Assisi, or incredibly bright like St. Augustine. We like saints with a bit of flash, given to visions, workers of miracles.

Judged from this perspective, Thérèse of Lisieux is a major disappointment. She never counseled the pope, fought in the arena, or bantered with the intelligentsia. She had an extremely limited, almost nonexistent, experience of phenomena such as visions and ecstasies. Worse yet, she said she wanted to be "forgotten... trod under foot like a grain of sand." In fact, she led a very sheltered life in the cultural confines of nineteenth-century bourgeois France. In just about every category, Thérèse comes up short.

Or maybe she doesn't. Perhaps the problem lies not with Thérèse or the other saints but with our expectations of them. We are an achievement-oriented society, focused on wealth, power, and accomplishment. Whether we intend to or not, many of us apply this same standard to the saints. It's not enough for them to be holy, they also have to found great missionary orders, convert enormous numbers of people, have visions, and die as martyrs.

It may be that we're more comfortable with the external and less sure of the internal. Regardless, there is no other standard with which to measure the saints than their inner life with God. Nothing matters less, when assessing the saints, than what they accomplished.

This is particularly true when considering Thérèse of Lisieux. Obviously, a woman who spent the last nine years of her life in a cloistered convent and died at the age of twenty-four didn't achieve much in worldly terms. She conquered herself and she attained union with God and that's about it. By the only standard that counts, the gospel, she was a phenomenal success.

The Cross behind the Flower

In spite of her low profile, Thérèse does enjoy a measure of popularity today and was quite a hit among Christians in the years immediately following her death. This was partially due to her startling deathbed promise to "spend my heaven doing good on earth." She was true to her word and as astonishing accounts of her intercession began to circulate, her fame spread.

Many people, too, found her "little way" of holiness, based on small sacrifices and acts of kindness, helpful in living the Christian life.

To a certain extent, however, Thérèse's popularity is based on a false reading of her life and personality. In the reverse of the typical situation, where we admire a saint for his or her accomplishments, Thérèse is admired for what is perceived as a childlike docility. No need to worry that Thérèse will nag about the poor or challenge authority or ask hard questions. She was sweet, submissive, and a saint to boot. Those who like their saints nonthreatening find this version of Thérèse satisfying.

Thérèse can indeed appear passive to those who give her a shallow reading or who encounter some of the sentimental material written about her. Her nickname, "The Little Flower," doesn't help. It may have been charming in nineteenth-century France, but today it conjures up images of a delicate helplessness at odds with our hard-edged culture. Even Thérèse's sister, Céline, had her doubts about the name. She was afraid that too many people failed to see the cross behind The Little Flower.

Thérèse is partially responsible for the misunderstanding. What are we to make of a saint who calls herself "the little toy of the baby Jesus"? More often than we'd like, she slips into this naive, excessively sweet prose. The reader occasionally needs considerable determination to plow through her letters and her autobiography, *The Story of a Soul*.

Actually, Thérèse's writing style is nothing more than a reflection of the French middle-class culture in which she grew up and her own youth. Nevertheless, it has earned her an unenviable and undeserved reputation as a lightweight.

Thomas Merton, the Trappist monk and author, said he was surprised, when he first became acquainted with Thérèse, to discover that she "was not just a mute, pious little doll in the imaginations of a lot of sentimental old women.... No sooner had I got a faint glimpse of the real character and the real spirituality of St. Thérèse, than I was immediately and strongly attracted to her.... Not only was she a saint," he concluded, "but a great saint, one of the greatest: tremendous!"

Thomas Merton was a cautious man with a probing intellect, never guilty of sentimentalism. Typical, in fact, of many today who are likely to dismiss Thérèse. Merton took a hard look, however, and liked what he saw. Undoubtedly, there is more to The Little Flower than either her name or her girlish reputation would imply.

The Fruit of Devout Parents

Thérèse Martin was born on January 2, 1873 in Alençon, France, the last of nine children. Much has been written about her remarkable parents, Louis and Zélie Guerin Martin, and they are under consideration for canonization themselves. Five of their children survived, all of them girls, and all of whom entered the convent.

Louis and Zélie, too, had originally hoped to enter the religious life. Louis set his sights on the Augustinian canons of the Great St. Bernard Hospice in the Alps. Together with their famous dogs, these monks rescued travelers lost in the snow or stranded on mountain passes. Their quiet way of life coupled with occasional feats of derring-do appealed to the young Martin.

Louis visited the hospice, but the prior told him to apply when he had learned Latin, necessary to a monastic career. Martin returned to his hometown of

Alençon and studied intensely for a year. Then, for unknown reasons, he gave up. It may be that he was unable to master Latin, he may have suffered from poor health, or he may simply have misjudged his vocation. At any rate, he turned to a career in watch-making and repair. He opened a shop in Alençon in 1850.

About this same time, Zélie, also a native of Alençon, learned that she, too, had no future in the religious life. In Zélie's case, however, she was rejected by the order to which she applied, the Sisters of St. Vincent de Paul. The mother superior gave no reason other than to say that Zélie didn't have a vocation.

This unexpected turn of events left Zélie adrift. She went to the Blessed Mother in prayer. One day she heard an interior voice very clearly say: "Go and make Point d'Alençon," the handmade lace for which Alençon was famous. Zélie learned the art and established herself in business. Within a few years she became enormously successful.

Louis and Zélie might have continued on their separate paths for years, successful, unmarried and pious, but for a combination of circumstances. Louis' mother was eager for him to marry and, having met Zélie, decided she was the woman for him.

For her part, Zélie one day happened to pass by a tall, serious man whose appearance struck her. Again, an interior voice spoke, saying: "This is the man you are going to marry." It turned out to be Louis Martin.

At this point, Louis' mother intervened, brought the two of them together, and they were soon married.

After this happy resolution, we would expect the Martins to begin producing children. However, the story takes an unusual twist. Louis and Zélie, in imitation of the Blessed Virgin and St. Joseph, decided to have a celibate marriage. Actually, the decision was probably more Louis' than Zélie's. She had prayed, on being rejected by the convent, that God would let her marry and bear many children. These would be consecrated to him.

Ten months after the wedding, a priest convinced the Martins to reverse their decision. Children followed in quick succession, to the parent's great delight. "I was born to have children," Zélie said from her lively home. "I'm mad about them."

By the time Thérèse arrived on the scene, the family had taken its final form. Marie was almost thirteen years old; Pauline was ten; Léonie, nine; and Céline, four. The Martins had endured the deaths of two infant sons, an infant daughter, and five-year-old Hélène, whom Zélie referred to as "a lovely jewel."

Pious but Real

For awhile, it looked as if Thérèse might soon follow her siblings into eternity. She rallied, though, and developed into a healthy, sturdy little girl. The high religious standards of the home and the deep affection of Louis and Zélie set the stage for the type of devout childhood we have come to expect of the saints. Thérèse doesn't let us down.

The writer Flannery O'Connor said that "stories of pious children tend to be false.... I have never cared to read about little boys who build altars and play they are priests, or about little girls who dress up as nuns, or about those pious Protestant children who lack this equipment but brighten the corners where they are."

In Thérèse's case, O'Connor was wrong about the stories being false. They are abundant and were confirmed by many witnesses during the canonization process. O'Connor may have been right when she implied that a stream of such stories tends to be tedious, if not unbelievable.

Thérèse was as good as children get, with a clear view of heaven and a great love of God. Still, she had spirit. Her mother described her as bright, mischievous, and "unconquerably stubborn." She had something of a temper and once stamped her foot at the maid and called her "a little brat." One has to look long and hard to find similar incidents.

Thérèse expressed herself in unusual ways. In a letter, her mother recounted a conversation she had with Thérèse when the child was three. "'Poor little mother,' [Thérèse] says, 'I do wish you'd die.' Then, when you scold her, she explains: 'Oh, but it's only because I want you to go to heaven. You told me yourself one can't go to heaven without dying.' She wants to kill off her father, too, when she gets really affectionate."

Unfortunately, Thérèse's hopes for her mother were realized much too soon. When Thérèse was four years old, Zélie Martin died of breast cancer. This marked the beginning of what Thérèse called the saddest period of her life, which lasted for ten years. She lost her happy disposition and became wary and oversensitive, crying at the least provocation. It wasn't until Thérèse was fourteen that she achieved the great interior victory that liberated her from hypersensitivity and launched her on the path to spiritual freedom.

A Father's Motherly Love

Psychology places great emphasis on the role of the father in forming a child's notion of God. An affectionate, supportive father is more likely to produce a secure child, able to experience God's love. In the aftermath of Zélie's death, Louis Martin fulfilled his role beyond any child's expectations.

"Daddy's affection seemed enriched by a real motherly love," Thérèse wrote in her autobiography.

They often went fishing together and he took her on walks, picnics, daily visits to the Blessed Sacrament, and little vacations to the sea or to visit friends. He called her his little queen, and though he was deeply devoted to her, managed to avoid spoiling her.

Thérèse speaks of him frequently. "I can't put into words how much I loved Daddy," she wrote. "I admired everything about him." After her work was done, she used to play by his side in the garden. "I got most fun out of soaking seeds and bits of bark in water and then offering the liquid to Daddy in a pretty little cup. He'd take it and smile and pretend to drink it."

He gave her a patch of garden where she grew flowers and decorated little altars in a niche in the wall. "When I'd finished," she recalled, "I'd run and fetch Daddy. He went into raptures of admiration to please me as he gazed at what I was sure were masterpieces. I should never end if I were to tell all the thousand and one memories I have of things like this. How can I tell of all the love Daddy showered on his little queen?"

The picture Thérèse paints is ideal and, according to her sisters, accurate. They were not jealous of her, they explained at the canonization proceedings, because their father was warm and affectionate with all of them. True, his love for his youngest daughter was unique, but they could see that Thérèse brought him great comfort.

The bond Louis forged with Thérèse was vital to her spiritual development. She was an incredibly secure individual with high self-esteem and remarkable confidence in God. Interestingly, however, this warm relationship did not spare Thérèse the tremendous aridity she experienced as a nun in her relationship with God.

Psychologically speaking, the strong love of her earthly father should have led Thérèse, as an adult, into a warm, lively relationship with her heavenly Father. The opposite is true. Although there was plenty of warmth on Thérèse's side, she generally met silence and even, toward the end, what felt like indifference from the other side.

Throughout her religious life, Thérèse had no consolation in prayer and no experience of God's presence. She felt nothing of an emotional nature to draw her forward in her vocation. During the last year and a half of her life, she lost her belief in heaven, and struggled with despair and doubt.

In short, in spite of a childhood soaked in love, Thérèse still had to make a leap of faith: God asked her to believe in him even though she didn't experience him. Thérèse's warm relationship with her father prepared her to make an intellectual assent to faith when the feelings were gone. It did not give her the sort of cozy experience of God we might have expected.

Crybaby No More

While Thérèse was basking in her father's love, her sisters, especially Pauline, were lavishing her with motherly love. On Zélie's death, Thérèse had asked Pauline to be her mother, and Céline, eight years old at the time, had asked Marie to be hers. Both these young women outdid themselves in their care for their little sisters. Even in her autobiography, Thérèse addresses Pauline as her "little mother."

Zélie's brother, Isidore Guerin, and his wife Céline, helped the Martin family cope. Soon after the funeral, the Martins moved to Les Buissonnets, a house in Lisieux near their cousins. An extremely happy relationship sprang up between these two pious families. One of the Guerin daughters, Marie, later joined the Martin girls in the Carmel at Lisieux.

Once again, however, Thérèse's world came crashing down: Pauline entered the Carmelite convent when Thérèse was almost ten years old. "Jesus took away from me that little mother whom I loved so dearly," Thérèse later lamented. "How can I express the agony I suffered. In a flash I understood what life was. Until then I had not seen it as too sad a business, but now I saw it as it really was–a thing of suffering and continual partings."

A few months later, in what may have been in part a psychological reaction to Pauline's departure,

Thérèse suffered a complete collapse. She hovered near death. Her father, in despair, arranged for a series of Masses to be said for her recovery at the shrine of Our Lady of Victories in Paris.

The family was devoted to Mary and a statue of Our Lady of Victories stood near Thérèse's bed. During the course of the novena, Thérèse took a turn for the worse. One day, however, when she looked at the statue, Mary smiled at her. Instantly, Thérèse recovered her health.

Unfortunately, the miraculous intervention caused a sensation. Thérèse was badgered by people who wanted to hear the details. The persistent questioning robbed her of her joy in the event, and she endured such humiliation over the experience that she could only regard herself with contempt. "Only in heaven shall I be able to tell what I suffered," she wrote.

All in all, Thérèse seems to have been a rather gloomy child during this period of her life. She attended school where she excelled academically but had trouble making friends. It's not difficult to see why. "I was cheerful enough," she said later, "but I didn't know how to play games, and so during playtime I often used to stand by a tree and think of serious matters. I invented a game which pleased me: I used to bury the poor little birds we found lying dead under the trees. Many of the girls helped me and our cemetery became very pretty...."

Later, Thérèse spoke of her difficulty making friends as a blessing. She had an ardent nature and an intense longing to be loved which she felt could have created problems. "It was only God's mercy that kept me from giving myself up to the love of creatures," she reflected. "Without that, I might have fallen as low as St. Mary Magdalene did.... Lucky for me that I had so little gift for making myself agreeable."

Thérèse may not have been the life of the party, but she was making remarkable spiritual progress. This was due to her own nature but also to the intense spirituality of her home. Marie, who prepared her for First Communion, was "so eloquent that her noble and generous spirit seemed to pass into mine. As the warriors of old trained their children in the profession of arms, so she trained me for the battle of life, and roused my ardor by pointing out the victor's glorious palm."

On the other hand, Marie was sensible. Thérèse told her that she wanted to practice mental prayer, but Marie said no. She was already devout enough. Thérèse had the last word, however. She used to go into a space behind her bed, shut off by a curtain. There she sat and thought about God, life, and eternity. "I realize now that I was engaged in mental prayer without knowing it," she wrote in her autobiography, "and that God was teaching me it in secret."

The pace of Thérèse's spiritual development quickened with the reception of her First Communion when she was eleven. On that occasion she achieved a mystical union with God, the type of experience that would soon be little more than a memory. She may have had a glimpse of the spiritual dryness that awaited her when she received Communion again not too long after.

On that occasion, she said, "[I was] seized with a passionate longing to suffer.... Until then, I had suffered without loving suffering. But from that day, I felt a deep true love for it." It was not because she loved pain. Rather, she knew the redemptive value of suffering, as demonstrated by Jesus on the cross.

She regarded this moment as one of the greatest graces of her life. Shortly after, she received Confirmation and, with it, "the strength to suffer. The martyrdom of my soul was about to start."

First, however, Thérèse had to overcome her tendency to be a "crybaby," as she frankly called herself. She had fought against this hypersensitivity for ten years, with little success.

"My extreme sensitiveness made me quite unendurable," she wrote. "If I ever offended anyone accidentally, instead of making the best of it I wept bitterly and so made things worse. Then, when I'd stopped weeping, I'd start all over again and weep for having wept.... I couldn't cure myself of this wretched fault." Her family, who must have gotten fed up with this behavior, told her that she cried so much as a child that she'd have no tears left to shed as an adult.

Her liberation came on Christmas Day, 1886, when she received what she called "the grace of conversion." The Martins had attended midnight Mass and returned to Les Buissonnets. According to tradition, Thérèse had left her shoes by the fireplace, expecting to find presents in them. Her father, thinking she was too old for this, became annoyed when he saw them. "Thank goodness it's the last time we shall have this sort of thing," he snapped.

Thérèse, headed upstairs to drop off her coat, overheard him. She hesitated, on the verge of tears. Céline urged her not to go back down, knowing that she would end up crying. But something was different and Thérèse knew it. In an instant, she later said, Jesus had changed her heart. She forced back her tears, entered the living room as though nothing had happened and joyfully opened her gifts. At that moment, she claimed, she regained the strength of soul she had lost when her mother died. She also recovered her happy disposition to such a degree that later, in the convent, she was known for her wit and sense of humor.

"On that night of nights began the third period of my life," Thérèse wrote, "the most beautiful and the most filled with graces from heaven. The work I had been unable to do in ten years was done by Jesus in one instant, contenting himself with my good will which was never lacking."

Thérèse received another significant grace at the same moment. "[God] made me a fisher of men," she declared. "I longed to work for the conversion of sinners with a passion I'd never felt before.... The cry of Jesus on the cross—'I am thirsty'—rang continually in my heart." She wanted to quench this thirst by presenting him with converted sinners. "I myself was consumed with a thirst for souls," Thérèse said.

As a sort of test of this new direction, she prayed for the conversion of an unrepentant murderer named Pranzini. The condemned man remained obdurate. Moments before his execution, however, he seized a crucifix offered him by a priest and kissed it three times. "After this striking favor," she commented, "my longing for souls grew greater every day."

With Courage and Persistence

Thérèse claimed that she wanted to be a nun from the age of three. Now that she was fourteen, she was convinced her time had come. Marie had joined Pauline in the Lisieux Carmel, and Léonie had made a brief, unsuccessful attempt to enter the Poor Clares.

Louis had willingly surrendered these daughters to

the religious life, but it had been difficult. It would be even more so with Thérèse, his favorite. Nevertheless, she summoned up her courage and on the feast of Pentecost, 1887, she approached her father for the necessary permission.

Perhaps this moment, more than any, validates Thérèse's immense regard for her father. She came upon him as he sat in the garden in the early evening sunlight, utterly at peace. There were tears in her eyes, and he held her close and asked what was troubling his "little queen." Perhaps Louis sensed what was to come for he got up "as if to hide his own emotion," Thérèse later said. He began to walk slowly up and down, holding her close to him. They both wept as she pleaded her case, but he was convinced of her vocation and made no attempt to discourage her. God honored him greatly, he said with feeling, by asking him to surrender his children.

Now that she had her father's permission, Thérèse thought no obstacles remained to thwart her entry into Carmel. She failed to take into account her age. The nuns themselves were ready to accept her, but that was not enough. First she had to persuade everyone from her Uncle Isidore to the bishop that she was indeed mature enough for the sacrifice.

Louis helped her apply to the proper authorities for permission to join the order and then took Thérèse and Céline off on a pilgrimage to Rome. If they couldn't resolve the problem before their departure, he said, he intended to have Thérèse speak to the pope himself. And so she did.

The great moment came on November 20, 1887. The members of the Martin's tour group crowded into the audience hall, each awaiting his turn to approach Pope Leo XIII to receive his blessing. They were "absolutely forbidden" to speak, a priest warned them, but Thérèse boldly stuck to her plan. She knelt before the pope, once again in tears. "Holy Father," she blurted, "I have a great favor to ask.... To mark your jubilee, allow me to enter Carmel at fifteen."

A hubbub broke out. One of the priests, quite irritated, told the pope that the matter was in the hands of the authorities. "Very well, my child," Pope Leo said to Thérèse, "do whatever they say." Thérèse had come a long way for this moment, and she was not about to be put off. She clasped her hands, placed them on the pope's knees and made a final effort. "O most Holy Father," she pleaded. "If you say yes, everybody will be only too willing." "Come, come," he responded, "you will enter if God wills." The determined Thérèse was about to speak again when two guards and a priest physically removed her.

Thérèse was in despair over what she perceived as her failed mission, but others were impressed by her courage and persistence. There was still some opposition to her request, but she surmounted the difficulties. On April 9, 1888, Thérèse entered the Lisieux Carmel at the age of fifteen.

In the Convent

Religious life was exactly as Thérèse expected. The prayers, the deprivations, the food, the chores, the nuns themselves–nothing surprised her. She made a smooth transition, but her vocation was immediately put to the test.

The prioress of the convent, Mother Marie de Gonzague, was a capable, efficient administrator but she had a difficult personality. She easily flew into a temper, criticized the other nuns, was jealous, self-important, and had no sympathy for the elderly, sick, or weak. Thérèse soon discovered that there were significant problems in the Carmel, most of which could be traced to the prioress.

Mother Marie had encouraged and welcomed Thérèse's entry, but to all appearances her enthusiasm waned once Thérèse was present. She was harsh and demanding. In her infrequent conferences with the young postulant, Mother Marie spent most of the time berating her. "She never met me without finding fault," Thérèse recalled. "I remember on one occasion when I had left a cobweb in the cloister, she said to me before the whole community: 'It is easy to see our cloisters are swept by a child of fifteen. It is disgraceful....' This was her invariable method of dealing with me."

Appearances to the contrary, the prioress was impressed with Thérèse. "I should never have believed such ripeness of judgment in someone of fifteen," she said. She felt that an individual of Thérèse's exceptional maturity and holiness should not be coddled. Thérèse accepted the ill-treatment out of obedience, but also because she genuinely loved Mother Marie. She felt that the prioress's method was the right one.

Thérèse's greatest source of suffering at this time was not Mother Marie but the rapid physical and mental decline of her father. He had suffered a small stroke prior to the pilgrimage to Rome. After Thérèse's entry into Carmel he endured a series of strokes that left him increasingly incapacitated. One day, he disappeared only to turn up a few days later at the harbor in Le Havre. The family placed him in a mental institution where, in his lucid moments, he was well aware of his fate.

"It is the worst trial a man can undergo," he said. His daughters drew comfort from the fact that he both accepted his condition and offered it up as a prayer. "I have never suffered a humiliation and I needed one," he told a doctor. "I am used to commanding and now I must obey."

He paid a last visit to Carmel shortly before he

died, his helpless body tucked into a wheelchair. "It was a sad interview," Thérèse said. "At the moment of parting he raised his eyes, then, pointing upwards, said in a voice choked with tears: 'In heaven,'" meaning they would meet again in heaven. He died in 1894.

Simply Love

All the elements of Thérèse's spirituality were in place when she entered the convent, needing only fuller development. Her approach was refreshingly straightforward and uncomplicated. A perceptive older nun once told Thérèse that her soul was very simple. "When you are perfect," the nun continued, "you will be more simple still. The nearer one gets to God, the simpler one becomes."

Still, Thérèse's path to sanctity sometimes looks simpler than it really is. Often it is reduced to nothing more than her "little way" with its small, daily acts of thoughtfulness and sacrifice. Thérèse, however, would have abandoned the little way in an instant if she had thought that was the sum of the spiritual life. What really mattered to Thérèse was God himself. The little way was simply the approach she used to love him and her neighbor.

It's difficult to do justice to Thérèse's intense, exclusive love for the Lord. "She breathed the love of God just as I breathe air," her sister Pauline said of her. Thérèse couldn't imagine what more she could enjoy after her death than she already enjoyed. "I know that I shall see the good Lord, but as far as being with him, I am already totally with him here on earth." She didn't experience him, we know, but she was with him in the sense that she was completely given over to his will.

Thérèse had an electrifying awareness of the importance of God's love for us and our love for him, particularly in the person of Jesus. "Jesus alone, no one but him," she declared. "O Jesus, may I never seek nor find anyone but you alone.... May you, Jesus, be everything!" She was overcome when she considered the enormity of his sacrifice on the cross. He had pushed his love to the extreme and she was determined to respond in kind.

Thérèse concluded that her vocation was, simply, love. She wanted to be everything for the Lord, from apostle to martyr, but realized that was impossible. "My vocation is love," she decided. "I understood that love comprised all vocations, that love was everything, that it embraced all times and places... in a word, that it was eternal!"

Thérèse put a different spin on this conclusion than we might expect. Her vocation included receiving God's love and giving it to others, which seems conventional enough. But she had a keen sense that God himself longed for our love. Many people either refused to give it to him or didn't realize how intensely he wanted it. God doesn't need that love, she knew, but nevertheless, he yearned for it.

With that in mind, Thérèse offered herself as a "victim" to this love. "In 1895 I was enabled to understand more clearly than ever before how Jesus longs to be loved," she recalled. Thérèse knew that some people offered themselves to God as victims of his justice, to draw his punishment away from sinners onto themselves. She wanted to draw down his mercy. "O my divine master, must it be only your justice which has its victims? Hasn't your merciful love need of them too? It is everywhere rejected and ignored."

She went ahead and made the offering. After that, she said, her life became "one act of perfect love. Since that day, I have been soaked and engulfed in love."

But not an experiential love. The great mystery of Thérèse's life, of course, is the utter silence God adopted after she entered the convent. She who had enjoyed God's warmth and compassion, now found herself abruptly cut off.

"A most complete dryness and a feeling that I was almost abandoned (by God), these were my portion," she said of her retreat before her profession. Of her thanksgivings after receiving Communion she claimed, "I have less consolation then than I ever have!" "Don't imagine that I'm overwhelmed with consolations," she wrote in a note to her sister, Marie. "I'm not. My consolation is not to have any in this life. Jesus never manifests himself nor lets me hear his voice."

Thérèse's response to this unexpected turn of events was nothing short of heroic. "Jesus does not want us to serve him for his gifts," she insisted. "It is he himself who must be our reward." She hadn't come to the convent to experience God or to feel good, she was there solely to love him and to win souls for him through her sacrifices. "I do not desire sensible affection, a love that I feel," she said, "but only a love that is felt by Jesus. Oh! To love him and to cause him to be loved!"

Thérèse's sufferings were not confined to her prayer life. The little way, so often misinterpreted as the mere performance of one's duties, was a daily exercise in martyrdom for Thérèse. Zélie had claimed that her daughter was "unconquerably stubborn." Thérèse retained that iron will throughout her life and bent it toward the service of others only at extreme cost to herself.

But bend it she did, countless times a day. Her sister Céline, who entered Carmel after Louis' death, provided an example. Thérèse used to hang around the other nuns after her work was done, Céline recalled. She wanted the sisters to feel free to ask for her help, which they invariably did. "This cost her a great deal," Céline said. She then gave an amusing insight into her own attitude when she added, "I often showed her how it could be avoided." Needless to say, Céline's tips were in vain. "[Thérèse] wanted to be at the beck and call of everybody."

Thérèse wasn't "naturally" disposed to lay down her life. She was able to do so only because she trained herself to do so day in and day out. She took advantage of even the smallest opportunities to die to herself–this is why her way is little–and found there sufficient material to achieve sanctity. This daily crucifixion gives the lie to those who perceive Thérèse as insipid.

Thérèse wasn't naturally inclined toward humility either, although it is a cornerstone of her little way. She took the virtue far beyond the common under-standing of humility as a modest opinion of oneself. She even went beyond the notion of being despised, insulted, or mocked. Thérèse wanted to be forgotten. Why? "The glory of my Jesus," she said, "that is all." Any attention that came to her would only detract from the glory due to him.

Like St. Paul, Thérèse actually took delight in her imperfections. "I willingly boast of my weaknesses," Paul said, for "in weakness power reaches perfection"

(2 Cor 12:9). If the other nuns discover your faults, so what? In fact, what a blessing! "You can then practice humility," Thérèse said, "which consists not only in thinking and saying that you are full of faults, but in rejoicing because others think and say the same thing about you."

Pain for the Conversion of Sinners

Thérèse was certainly more than "a pious little doll," more than the demure child of overwrought imaginations. She had the advantage of a secure childhood but that didn't spare her the total interior stripping she endured as a nun. A barren prayer life? Ill-tempered nuns? Insufficient food? An unbalanced mother superior? Thérèse waded into the fray with gusto and displayed a measure of self-control and charity that was astonishingly close to perfect.

Perhaps nothing brings her closer to the soul of the twentieth century, however, than the last year and a half of her life. As if anticipating the doubts that would plague future generations, Thérèse experienced an almost complete loss of faith. She struggled with outright disbelief until the moment of her death.

This dark night of the soul came upon her unexpectedly. During Lent of 1896, she had twice vomited blood, a harbinger of the tuberculosis that would eventually kill her. She was delighted at the thought of her approaching death. "In those days my faith was so clear and vigorous that I found perfect happiness in the thought of heaven." Not for long.

"[Jesus] allowed pitch-black darkness to sweep over my soul and let the thought of heaven, so sweet to me from my infancy, destroy all my peace and torture me," she lamented. Her soul was "smothered," she said, and she couldn't even imagine a place like heaven. "Everything about it had vanished!"

In one of the most poignant passages of her autobiography, Thérèse wrote that the voice of unbelievers mocked her from the darkness. "Hope on! Hope on! And look forward to death!" they jeered. "But it will give you, not what you hope for, but a still darker night, the night of annihilation!"

At the same time, Thérèse began a long, agonizing physical decline that led to unimaginable suffering. "Never would I have believed it was possible to suffer so much! Never! Never!" she cried. The last few months were a nightmare of pain, unrelieved by sedatives. Mother Marie, true to form, thought a Carmelite ought to be able to handle a bit of suffering.

Thérèse could. This was in part because she longed to be a martyr, but primarily because she wanted to offer her pain for the conversion of sinners. This thirst for souls was the only explanation she could give for her suffering. Thérèse endured it all with her customary serenity and joy, leading the doctor to pronounce her "an angel."

Still, it was a difficult business. She found her trial of faith incomprehensible. Nor did she have the consolation of sharing her thoughts. "She didn't speak about it to anyone for fear of communicating her inexpressible torment to others," Céline said after Thérèse's death.

Thérèse triumphed, in a staggering display of self-control and complete submission to the will of God. Stripped of all solace, she realized that in the end she simply had to trust in God. "My agony may reach the furthest limits, but I am convinced he will never forsake me. We can never have too much confidence in God." She didn't regret those words even as her final slide toward death began. On September 29, the day before she died, she cried out: "I can't take any more! Pray for me!" Shortly after, however, she pulled herself together and said: "Yes, God, I want it all."

Her last agony began on the afternoon of September 30th. "Her features were contracted, her hands purple, her feet were icy cold and she trembled in every limb," Pauline wrote. "The death sweat stood out in great drops on her forehead and coursed down her face. The ever increasing oppression made her utter feeble involuntary cries in her efforts to breathe." "It's pure suffering," Thérèse said, "because there isn't any consolation in it. No, not one."

The nuns had been gathered around her bed in prayer, but Mother Marie sent them away when it seemed Thérèse was holding her own. "Oh, Mother," Thérèse cried out, "is it not yet the agony, am I not going to die?" Mother Marie said that it might be a few more hours. "Well, all right, all right," Thérèse responded. "I wouldn't want to suffer less. Oh, I love him. My God, I love you."

With that, Thérèse fell back gently, and Mother Marie hastily reassembled the nuns. Thérèse's face was transformed by a look of great joy. "Suddenly, she sat up," Céline recounted, "as if a mysterious voice had called her. She opened her eyes and fixed them radiantly on a spot a little above the statue of Our Lady. She stayed that way for a few minutes, about as long as it would take to recite the Credo slowly." Then she closed her eyes and died.

A Saint for Modern Times

Many nuns live holy lives, die holy deaths, and are forgotten. Thérèse knew her name would endure. Her autobiography would do much good, she said, and she warned her sisters to publish it promptly after her death. "If there is any delay," she warned, "… the devil will set a thousand snares to prevent its publication—and it is important that it should be published. It will help all kinds of souls."

Initially, the book had not been written for publication. Pauline, during a term as prioress, had asked Thérèse to write down her memories of her childhood, as a sort of keepsake for the family. Later, at Pauline's urging, Mother Marie ordered Thérèse to continue the story which she completed three months before her death.

The Story of a Soul was published a year later, and Thérèse's words proved prophetic. The book swept the world. Within a few years reports of miracles attributed to her intercession began to flood Rome. A clamor arose for her canonization, and the process was completed in twenty-eight years—an extraordinarily speedy accomplishment.

Thérèse has been remembered, too, because she seems determined not to be forgotten. Not for her own sake, but for ours. "If God answers my desires," she said, "my heaven will be spent on earth until the end of the world. Yes, I want to spend my heaven in doing good on earth." She promised that she would let fall "a shower of roses," answers to prayer.

Thérèse has been as good as her word, which comes as no surprise. The church teaches that there is an ongoing relationship between those who have died and the faithful on earth. This communion of saints means that our responsibility to one another doesn't end with death. The saints in heaven intercede for the faithful on earth, the faithful on earth pray for the souls in purgatory. We're all in it for the long haul.

Thérèse has made her intentions abundantly clear in this regard. A sheltered nun who died young may seem an odd saint for modern times. But Thérèse accomplished two feats that elude many in our over-stimulated culture: she conquered herself, and she developed a clear understanding of the nature of love. She stands ready to help others do the same.

"Don't worry about impressive achievements," Thérèse would say if we could talk to her today. "They don't amount to much. Love God. Serve your neighbor. Avoid sin. Stay humble."

And ask Thérèse to lend a hand. She won't disappoint.

ONE

To Love Him and to Be Loved by Him

ONE DAY WHEN Thérèse was three or four years old, she and her sister Céline were playing together. Their older sister, Léonie, deciding she was too old for dolls, brought a basketful of her doll clothing and accessories to the younger girls. She told them to take what they wanted. Céline took a little bundle of silk braid, but Thérèse declared, "I choose everything!" "Without further ado," she records, "I carried off the lot."

The incident is vintage Thérèse. She was a shoot–for–the–moon sort of individual. When she wanted something, whether doll clothes as a child or humility as an adult, she went after it full tilt.

Most of all, Thérèse wanted the love of God. This was "everything" to her, the key to her spirituality and the core of her existence. To love him and to be loved by him made all other sacrifices possible.

Like many saints, Thérèse speaks with passion and intensity about the love of God. Referring to Jesus, she said that she wanted to "love him unto folly... more than he had ever been loved." He was "my first, my only friend," she wrote, "the one and only one whom I loved; he was my all."

Nothing could keep her from him—not sin, not fear of his justice, not discouragement, or personal weakness. "When, with childlike confidence, we cast our faults into the devouring furnace of Love, how can they fail to be consumed forever?" Thérèse asked.

If we repent for sin, that act of love repairs everything, she said. "Jesus opens his heart to us. He forgets our infidelities and does not want to recall them."

"[Thérèse] had such loving confidence in our Lord that her demands had a kind of limitless audacity," her sister Pauline said. "When she thought of his all-powerful love she had no uncertainty." "My way is not the way of fear," Thérèse agreed. "... [It is] full of confidence and love."

Even in the face of incredible suffering, she maintained her conviction. Her last words, uttered when she could barely speak and was in extreme pain, were, "Oh, I love him.... My God, I love you."

Suffering, Love, and Abandonment

Thérèse wanted to suffer both to prove her love for God and to do penance for the souls of sinners. As she matured, however, she focused less on suffering and more on abandonment to the will of God.

I have no other desire except to love Jesus unto folly. My childish desires have all flown away.... Neither do I desire any longer suffering or death, and still I love them both; it is love alone that attracts me, however. I desired them both for a long time; I possessed suffering and believed I had touched the shores of heaven....

Now, abandonment alone guides me. I have no other compass! I can no longer ask for anything with fervor except the accomplishment of God's will in my soul without any creature being able to set obstacles in the way. I can speak these words of the Spiritual Canticle of St. John of the Cross:

> In the inner wine cellar
> I drank of my beloved, and when I went abroad
>   Through all this valley
> I no longer knew anything,
> And lost the herd which I was following.
>
>   Now I occupy my soul
> And all my energy in his service;
>   I no longer tend the herd,
> Nor have I any other work
> Now that my every act is love.

We have only the short moments of our life to love Jesus, and the devil knows this well, and so he tries to consume our life in useless works....

Ever since I have been given the grace to understand also the love of the heart of Jesus, I admit that it has expelled all fear from my heart. The remembrance of my faults humbles me, reminds me never to draw on my strength which is only weakness, but this remembrance speaks to me of mercy and love even more.

When we cast our faults with entire filial confidence into the devouring fire of love, how would these not be consumed beyond return?

I know there are some saints who spent their life in the practice of astonishing mortifications to expiate their sins, but what of it: "There are many mansions in the house of my heavenly Father," Jesus has said, and it is because of this that I follow the way he is tracing out for me.

I try to be no longer occupied with myself in anything, and I abandon myself to what Jesus sees fit to do in my soul, for I have not chosen an austere life to expiate my faults but those of others.

Jesus is a hidden treasure, a good beyond price that few souls can find, for it is hidden and the world loves things that glitter. Ah! If Jesus had chosen to show himself to all souls with his ineffable gifts, surely not one would have spurned him. But he does not want us to love him for his gifts; it is himself that must be our reward.

It is not because I have been preserved from mortal sin that I fly to God with loving confidence. I know I should still have this confidence even if my conscience were burdened with every possible crime. I should fling myself into the arms of my savior, heartbroken with sorrow.

I know how he loved the prodigal son; I have heard his words to St. Mary Magdalene, to the woman taken in adultery, and to the woman of Samaria. No, no one could frighten me, for I know what to think about his love and his mercy.

I know that a host of sins would vanish in the twinkling of an eye like a drop of water flung into a furnace.

My God, you know that the only thing I've ever wanted is to love you; I have no ambition for any other glory except that. In my childhood, your love was there waiting for me; as I grew up, it grew with me; and now it is like a great chasm whose depths are past sounding.

Love breeds love; and mine, Jesus, for you, keeps on thrusting out towards you, as if to fill up that chasm which love has made—but it's no good;

mine is something less than a drop of dew lost in the ocean.

Love you as you love me? The only way to do that is to come to you for the loan of your own love. I couldn't content myself with less.

Dear Jesus, I can have no certainty about this, but I don't see how you could squander more love on a human soul than you have on mine! That's why I venture to ask that these souls you have entrusted to me [the novices in Thérèse's care] may experience your love as I have.

One day, maybe, in heaven, I shall find out that you love them better than me, and I shall be glad of that, glad to think that these people earned your love better than I ever did. But, here on earth, I just don't find it possible to imagine a greater wealth of love than the love you've squandered on me without my doing anything to earn it.

… All is fleeting that we cherish here under the sun. The only good thing is to love God with all one's heart and to stay poor in spirit.

A Victim of God's Love

Thérèse had heard of people who offered themselves to God as "victims" of his justice, in order to turn away his punishment from sinners, taking that punishment on themselves. She admitted that she was not attracted to this. Instead, Thérèse decided to offer herself as a victim of God's love in order to draw that love down upon the world.

O my God! Will your justice alone find souls willing to immolate themselves as victims? Does not your merciful love need them too? On every side this love is unknown, rejected.

Those hearts upon whom you would lavish it turn to creatures seeking happiness from them with their miserable affection. They do this instead of throwing themselves into your arms and accepting your infinite love.

O my God! Is your disdained love going to remain closed up within your heart? It seems to me that if you were to find souls offering themselves as victims of holocaust to your love, you would consume them rapidly. It seems to me, too, that you would be happy not to hold back the waves of infinite tenderness within you.

If your justice loves to release itself, this justice which extends only over the earth, how much more does your merciful love desire to set souls on fire since your mercy reaches to the heavens.

O my Jesus, let me be this happy victim. Consume your holocaust with the fire of your divine love!

Thérèse received permission from her mother superior, whom she addresses here, to offer herself as a victim of God's love [see preceding excerpt]. Although she was destined to endure intense suffering, she never regretted her decision.

It was you, dear Mother, who gave me leave to offer myself in this way, and you know all about the streams of grace, or perhaps I ought to say the seas of grace, which have come flooding into my soul since then.

Ever since that memorable day, love seems to pierce me through and wrap me round, merciful love which makes a new creature of me, purifies my soul and leaves no trace of sin there, till all my fear of Purgatory is lost.

To be sure, no merits of my own could even win me entrance there; it is only for the souls of the redeemed. But at the same time I felt confident that the fire of love can sanctify us more surely than those fires of expiation....

There's nothing that can bring us comfort like this way of love. For me, nothing matters except trying to do God's will with utter resignation.

When Thérèse offered herself to God's love, she experienced an overwhelming mystical sign of his acceptance. She described the moment for her sister, Marie.

I was commencing the Stations of the Cross in the choir that day when, suddenly, I felt that I had been wounded by a dart of fire so ardent that death must be near. I have no words to describe it; it was as though an invisible hand had plunged me into fire. And such fire! Yet at the same time, what sweetness! I was burning up with love and was convinced that to withstand such an onslaught of love for one minute, nay for even one second more, was impossible. Death must surely ensue.

It was an experimental knowledge of those states described by the saints and which some of them had so frequently experienced. But such a grace was mine only once—and even then, for one instant only. Almost immediately after, I fell back into my habitual state of aridity.

Oh, what a comfort it is, this way of love! You may stumble on it, you may fail to correspond with grace given, but always love knows how to make the best of everything. Whatever offends our Lord is burnt up in its fire, and nothing is left but a humble, absorbing peace deep down in the heart.

God's Justice—an Aspect of His Love

God's justice, Thérèse said, is simply another aspect of his love. We need not fear it since it flows from his infinite compassion for his children. In the next two excerpts, Thérèse reflects on this justice.

I know one must be very pure to appear before the God of all holiness, but I know, too, that the Lord is infinitely just; and it is this justice which frightens so many souls which is the object of my joy and confidence.

To be just is not only to exercise severity in order to punish the guilty; it is also to recognise right intentions and to reward virtue. I expect as much from God's justice as from his mercy.

It is because he is just that "he is compassionate and filled with gentleness, slow to punish and abundant in mercy, for he knows our frailty, he remembers we are only dust. As a father has tenderness for his children, so the Lord has compassion on us."

Thérèse felt that God guided her and gave her great graces through Scripture and through his presence within her. These unsought inspirations caused her to reflect on his love and justice.

… After receiving such graces, do you wonder that I should echo the words of the Psalmist: "Give thanks to the Lord. The Lord is gracious, his mercy endures forever."

I believe that if all creatures had received these same graces, there would be nobody left serving God under the influence of fear. We should all love him to distraction and nobody would ever do him an injury, not because we were afraid of him but simply because we loved him.

Still, I realise that we aren't all made alike. Souls have got to fall into different groups so that all God's perfections may be honored severally.

Only for me his infinite mercy is the quality that stands out in my life, and when I contemplate and adore his other perfections, it's against this background of mercy all the time. They all seem to have a dazzling outline of love. Even God's justice, and perhaps his justice more than any other attribute of his, seems to have love for its setting.

It's so wonderful to think that God is really just, that he takes all our weakness into consideration, that he knows our frail nature for what it is. What reason can I have for fear? Surely he who pardons so graciously the faults of the Prodigal Son will be equally just in his treatment of myself, who am always at his side.

One evening, not knowing how to tell Jesus that I loved him and how much I desired that he be loved and glorified everywhere, I was thinking that he would never receive a single act of love from hell. Then I said to God that to please him I would consent to see myself plunged into hell so that he would be loved eternally in that place of blasphemy.

I realised that this could not give him glory since he desires only our happiness, but when we love we experience the need of saying a thousand foolish things.

If I talked in this way, it wasn't because heaven did not excite my desire, but because at this time my heaven was none other than love and I felt, as did St. Paul, that nothing could separate us from the divine being who so ravished me!

All the great truths of religion, the mysteries of eternity, plunged my soul into a state of joy not of this earth. I experienced already what God reserved for those who love him (not with the eye but with the heart)....

Seeing the eternal rewards had no proportion to life's small sacrifices, I wanted to love, to love Jesus with a passion, giving him a thousand proofs of my love while it was possible.

Thinking Only of God's Pleasure

It was the custom of the Carmelites for each sister to compose a letter to the Lord and to carry it with her when she made her vows. Thérèse's letter encompasses many of her virtues, such as humility and zeal, but it was motivated by her immense love of God.

Jesus, my heavenly bridegroom, never may I lose this second robe of baptismal innocence. Take me to yourself before I commit any wilful fault, however slight. May I look for nothing and find nothing but you and you only. May creatures mean nothing to me nor I to them—you, Jesus, are to be everything to me.

May earthly things have no power to disturb the peace of my soul. That peace is all I ask of you, except love; love that is as infinite as you are, love that has no eyes for myself but for you Jesus, only for you.

Jesus, I would like to die a martyr for your sake, a martyr in soul or in body; better still, in both. Give me the grace to keep my vows in their entirety. Make me understand what is expected of one who is your bride.

Let me never be a burden to the community, never claim anybody's attention. I want them all to think of me as no better than a grain of sand, trampled underfoot and forgotten, Jesus, for your sake.

May your will be perfectly accomplished in me, till I reach the place you have gone to prepare for me. Jesus, may I be the means of saving many souls. Today, in particular, may no soul be lost, may all those detained in purgatory win release.

Pardon me, Jesus, if I am saying more than I've any right to; I'm thinking only of your pleasure, of your content.

Many serve Jesus when he consoles them, but few are willing to keep company with Jesus sleeping on the waves or suffering in the garden of agony.... Who then will be willing to serve Jesus for himself!

I know no other means to arrive at perfection save love.... Love, how evidently our heart is made for that!... Sometimes I try to find another word to express love, but on this earth of exile words are impotent to render all the vibrations of the soul, so one must rest satisfied with the single word Love!

... How easy it is to give pleasure to Jesus, to enrapture his heart! All one has to do is love him, not considering oneself, not examining one's faults too closely.

Take Jesus by the Heart

"[Thérèse] loved God as a child loves his father," one of her fellow nuns said of her, "and used the most unexpected ways to express her affection." Here Thérèse speaks with her customary simplicity and confidence.

… I find perfection quite easy to practice because I have realised that all one has to do is take Jesus by the heart.

Consider a small child who has displeased his mother, by flying into a rage or perhaps disobeying her. If he sulks in a corner and screams in fear of punishment, his mother will certainly not forgive his fault. But if he comes to her with his little arms outstretched, smiling and saying: "Kiss me, I won't do it again," surely his mother will immediately press him tenderly to her heart, forgetting all that he has done….

Of course, she knows quite well that her dear little boy will do it again at the first opportunity but that does not matter. If he takes her by the heart, he will never be punished….

Abandonment to His Will

On a practical level, Thérèse's love for God found expression in her complete acceptance of his will. This abandonment guided everything she did, from accepting suffering to faithfully carrying out her duties.

This saying of Job: "Although he should kill me, I will trust in him," has fascinated me from my childhood. But it took me a long time before I was established in this degree of abandonment. Now I am there; God has placed me there. He took me into his arms and placed me there.

My heart is filled with God's will, and when someone pours something on it, this doesn't penetrate its interior. It's a nothing which glides off easily, just like oil which can't mix with water. I remain always at profound peace in the depths of my heart. Nothing can disturb it.

The Folly of Divine Love

In a letter to Céline, Thérèse comments on the folly of divine love.

The one crime charged against Jesus by Herod was that he was mad. And I agree with him! Yes, it was folly to seek the poor little hearts of mortals to make them his thrones, he, the king of glory, who is throned above the cherubim! He whose presence is mightier than the heavens can contain!

Our beloved was mad to come down to earth seeking sinners to make them his friends, his intimates, to make them like unto himself, when he was perfectly happy with the two adorable persons of the Trinity.

We shall never be able to commit the follies for him that he has committed for us, nor do our actions deserve the name of folly, for they are in fact most reasonable acts, far below what our love would like to accomplish.

So that it is the world which is stupid, not realising what Jesus has done to save it. It is the world which is the all-devouring thing, seducing souls and leading them to fountains without water....

Reflection

Many of us grapple with fear in our lives–fear of sin, fear of suffering, fear of death, fear of failure, fear of war, fear that our sins will be found out. The list is endless. We live in an atmosphere of dread that is incompatible with the gospel and undermines our faith.

Thérèse was not afraid of anything. She loved God, he loved her and that was enough. The same can be true for us if we take God at his word and believe the good news. "Perfect love casts out all fear" (1 Jn 4:18).

Prayer

Lord, I know I don't grasp the depth of your love for me. Free me from everything that holds me back from receiving you. Let me love you without fear, knowing that you hold me in the palm of your hand. Through Christ our Lord. Amen.

TWO

The Cost of Loving One's Neighbor

G.K. CHESTERTON ONCE SAID of St. Francis of Assisi: "He was a lover of God and he was really and truly a lover of men, possibly a much rarer mystical vocation." The same is true of Thérèse of Lisieux.

Thérèse loved God passionately, as we might expect of a nun in a cloistered convent. But she loved her neighbor with equal zeal, a more difficult virtue to sustain. Far from isolating her, convent life was in some ways a more intense experience of ordinary life: difficult personalities and petty problems were literally inescapable within the confines of the cloister.

She tackled the situation with her customary determination. "Without love all we do is worthless," Thérèse said flatly. To dispel any illusions about the cost involved, she added: "The only thing that can be called love is the complete sacrifice of oneself."

Thérèse made that sacrifice to an extraordinary degree in the very ordinary circumstances of daily life. On some level, however, anybody can do what she did, as the following examples illustrate.

Thérèse insisted that if we take the first step, God will give us the grace necessary to love those around us. Often this means nothing more than offering a kind word or a helping hand when we don't feel like it.

Initially, Thérèse herself found such small challenges difficult. "At first," she said, "my face often betrayed the struggle I was having but gradually spontaneous self-sacrifice came easily.... For every grace I made good use of, he gave me many more." Still, she noted, there were occasions when she had to take her courage in both hands in order to avoid snapping at someone.

Thérèse recognized that love of neighbor is an essential ingredient of the gospel, however impossible the task may seem. She never implied it would be easy. At times, in fact, she practiced the virtue as a sort of martyrdom. Still, she stuck with it and she urged her readers to do the same.

Thérèse found support for her tenacity in one of her favorite quotes from St. John of the Cross: "The smallest movement of pure love is more useful to the church than all other works put together."

The Jesus in Others

From time to time, most of us find ourselves in situations with someone whose appearance or speech or personality irritate us. One particular nun had this effect on Thérèse. Here's how she handled it.

I reminded myself that charity isn't a matter of fine sentiments; it means doing things. So I determined to treat this sister as if she were the person I loved best in the world. Every time I met her, I used to pray for her, offering to God all her virtues and her merits....

But I didn't confine myself to saying a lot of prayers for her, this sister who made life such a tug-of-war for me; I tried to do her every good turn I possibly could.

When I felt tempted to take her down with an unkind retort, I would put on my best smile instead, and try to change the subject. Doesn't *The Imitation [of Christ]* tell us that it's better to let other people have their way in an argument, than to go on wrangling over it? We used often to meet outside recreation time, over our work; and when the struggle was too much for me I used to turn tail and run.

She was quite unconscious of what I really felt about her, and never realized why I behaved as I did. To this day, she is persuaded that her personality somehow attracts me. Once at recreation she actually said, beaming all over, something like this: "I wish you would tell me, Sister Thérèse of the

Child Jesus, what is it about me that gets the right side of you? You've always got a smile for me whenever I see you."

Well, of course, what really attracted me about her was Jesus hidden in the depths of her soul; Jesus makes the bitterest mouthful taste sweet. I could only say that the sight of her always made me smile with pleasure. Naturally I didn't explain that the pleasure was entirely spiritual.

The most trivial work, the least action when inspired by love, is often of greater merit than the most outstanding achievement. It is not on our face value that God judges our deeds, even when they bear the stamp of apparent holiness, but solely on the measure of love we put into them.

We should judge our neighbor favorably in every circumstance… and make it become a habit of ours to overlook his faults. Just as we—almost spontaneously—give ourselves the benefit of the doubt, let us also make this an integral factor of our relations with those about us.

It Didn't Come Easily

Love of neighbor didn't come easily to Thérèse. She had to work at it, just like the rest of us. However, her fierce determination to conquer herself and love those around her sets her apart from the ordinary Christian. This simple example should strike a chord for all those who have ever endured the whispering or coughing of others at church or a concert or movie.

At meditation I was for a long time always near a sister who never stopped fidgeting, with either her rosary or something else. Perhaps I was the only one who heard her, as my ears are very sharp, but I could not tell you how it irritated me.

What I wanted to do was to turn and stare at her until she stopped her noise, but deep down I knew it was better to endure it patiently—first, for the love of God and, secondly, so as not to upset her. So I made no fuss, though sometimes I was soaked with sweat under the strain and my prayer was nothing but the prayer of suffering.

At last I tried to find some way of enduring this suffering calmly and even joyfully. So I did my best to enjoy this unpleasant little noise. Instead of trying not to hear it—which was impossible—I strove to listen to it carefully as if it were a first-class concert, and my meditation, which was not the prayer of quiet, was spent in offering this concert to Jesus.

True charity consists in putting up with all one's neighbor's faults, never being surprised by his weakness, and being inspired by the least of his virtues.

If... the devil tries to show me the faults of a sister, I hasten to think of all her virtues and of how good her intentions are. I tell myself that though I have seen her commit a sin, she may very well have won many spiritual victories of which I know nothing because of her humility. What seems a fault to me may very well be an act of virtue because of the intention behind it.

Befriending the Imperfect

In the Gospel of Luke, Jesus tells his followers to take special care of the needy. "Whenever you give a lunch or dinner, do not invite your friends.... Invite beggars, and the crippled, the lame and the blind. You should be pleased that they cannot repay you."

Thérèse applied these words to some of her fellow nuns who, for one reason or another, had difficult personalities. Her approach is a striking example of the gospel in action.

I have noticed that the holiest nuns are the most loved. Other people want to talk to them and perform unasked services for them....

But imperfect souls have no friends. They are

treated with the ordinary politeness of convent life but they are avoided, for one is afraid of saying something unfriendly.

When I talk of imperfect souls, I am not referring only to spiritual imperfections, for the holiest person will be holy only in heaven. I also have in mind such things as lack of judgment and education and a general touchiness of disposition. They are all things which do nothing to make life pleasant. I am well aware that these are chronic disabilities and there is no hope of curing them....

From all this I have come to the conclusion that I should seek the company of those sisters for whom I have no natural liking and be like the Good Samaritan to them. A word and a pleasant smile are often enough to cheer up someone who is sad and upset.

But I want to be charitable not only to comfort people. I know I should soon lose heart if that were my aim, for something uttered with the best of intentions can, perhaps, be completely misunderstood. Therefore, to save time and trouble, I try to act solely to please our Lord.

Love, above All Else

Thérèse had been ordered by her superiors to write her autobiography. As her illness progressed, this became very difficult for her physically. The constant in-

terruptions of the other nuns, however, proved more of
a trial than her dwindling strength. Parents of young
children—anyone subjected to frequent interruptions—
can identify with Thérèse's dilemma.

Her solution? Love, above all else. Thérèse simply
put aside what she was doing and gave each sister her
undivided attention.

Her dry sense of humor comes into play as she de-
scribes a typical day. Thérèse is sitting in the garden in
a wheelchair while the other nuns bring in the hay.

When I begin to take up my pen, behold, a sister
passes by, a pitchfork on her shoulder. She believes
she will distract me with a little idle chatter: hay,
ducks, hens, visits of the doctor, everything is dis-
cussed.

To tell the truth, this doesn't last a long time, but
there is more than one good charitable sister, and
all of a sudden another hay worker throws flowers
on my lap, perhaps believing these will inspire me
with poetic thoughts. I am not looking for them at
the moment and would prefer to see the flowers
remain swaying on their stems....

I don't know if I have been able to write ten lines
without being disturbed... however, for the love of
God and my sisters (so charitable towards me) I take
care to appear happy and especially to be so.

For example, here is a hay worker who is just
leaving me after having said very compassionately:

"Poor little sister, it must tire you out writing like that all day long." "Don't worry," I answer, "I appear to be writing very much, but really, I am writing almost nothing." "Very good!" she says, "But just the same, I am very happy we are doing the haying since this always distracts you a little."

In fact, it is such a great distraction for me... that I am not telling any lies when I say that I am writing practically nothing.

Ah! What peace floods the soul when she rises above natural feelings.

Thérèse wanted to be everything for the Lord—a martyr, a priest, a saint, a missionary, an evangelist. Tormented by these unfulfilled longings, she sought an answer in the epistles of Paul. In 1 Corinthians 12 she read that the church has many members performing a variety of functions, not all can be prophets or apostles or evangelists.

That was a clear answer, but it failed to provide a focus for her yearnings. Reading on, she came upon Paul's famous passage on love in 1 Corinthians 13. At last, Thérèse felt, she had found the key to her vocation.

All the gifts of heaven, even the most perfect of them, without love, are absolutely nothing. Charity is the best way of all because it leads straight to God....

When St. Paul was talking about the different members of the mystical body, I couldn't recognize myself in any of them; or rather I could recognize myself in all of them. But charity—that was the key to my vocation.

If the church was a body composed of different members, it couldn't lack the noblest of all; it must have a heart, and a heart burning with love. And I realized that this love was the true motive force which enabled the other members of the church to act. If it ceased to function the apostles would forget to preach the gospel, the martyrs would refuse to shed their blood. Love, in fact, is the vocation which includes all others....

I had discovered where it is that I belong in the church, the niche God has appointed for me. To be nothing else than love, deep down in the heart of mother church. That's to be everything at once— my dream wasn't a dream after all.

To love your neighbor as yourself—that was the rule our Lord laid down before the Incarnation. He knew what a powerful motive self-love was and he could find no higher standard by which to measure the love of one's neighbor.

But this wasn't the "new commandment" Jesus gave to his disciples, his own commandment as he calls it.... I am not just to love my neighbors as myself. I am to love them as Jesus loves them and will love them till the end of time ["This is my commandment: love one another as I have loved you" (Jn 15:12)].

Dear Lord, you never tell us to do what is impossible, and yet you can see more clearly than I do how weak and imperfect I am. If, then, you tell me to love my sisters as you love them, that must mean that you yourself must go on loving them in and through me. You know it wouldn't be possible in any other way.

There would be no new commandment if you hadn't meant to give me the grace to keep it. How I welcome it, then, as proof that your will is to love, in and through me, all the people you tell me to love.

Always, when I act as charity bids, I have this feeling that it is Jesus who is acting in me. The closer my union with him, the greater my love for all the sisters without distinction.

Loving the Unlovable

Sister St. Peter, an elderly invalid, needed help every evening to get from church to the dining room. She was a crabby, hard-to-please nun, so no one was eager to volunteer. Thérèse took on the job, remembering the words of the Gospel: "As often as you did it for one of my least brothers, you did it for me."

Every evening, as soon as I saw her start shaking her hourglass, I knew it meant: "Let's start." Screwing up my courage, I got up and then quite a ceremony began. Before we set out, her stool had to be picked up and carried in a particular way. Above all, there had to be no sign of haste.

I had to follow her, supporting her.... If, however, she unfortunately stumbled, she instantly thought I was not holding on to her properly and that she was going to fall: "Oh, good heavens! You are walking too fast. I shall tumble down."

Then, if I tried to lead her more slowly, I would hear: "Keep close to me. I can't feel your hand. You've let go. I'm going to fall! I knew very well you were far too young to look after me."

We would finally arrive in the refectory without any accident. Fresh troubles began there. I had to settle the poor invalid in her place and it had to be done carefully so as not to hurt her. Her sleeves had to be turned back, too, again in a particular way. That done, I could go.

But I soon noticed that she found it very difficult to cut her bread, and so I used not to leave her without doing it for her. She was very touched by this, as she had never asked me to do it. I won her complete trust through this and especially—as I discovered much later—because at the end of all my little duties I gave her what she called "my nicest smile."

Generosity of the Heart

Thérèse felt that there should be no limits to generosity. She shrewdly pointed out, however, that the attitude of the giver is even more important than the act of giving.

... Our Lord has said: "What credit is it to you, if you lend to those from whom you expect repayment? Even sinners lend to sinners, to receive as much in exchange. No, you must lend without any hope of return. Then your reward will be a rich one."

A rich one, even here on earth. On this path of generosity, it's only the first step that takes it out of you. To lend without expecting to see your money back—that does go against the grain. You would rather give the thing outright, and see it pass out of your possession.

Someone comes up to you and says, with an air of complete assurance: "Dear sister, could you give me some help for an hour or two? It's all right, I've got Reverend Mother's leave to give you some of my own time in return. I know how busy you are."

Knowing, as you do, that she won't really repay the loan of your time, you're tempted to say: "Not at all. I'll make you a gift of it." That would gratify one's self-esteem. A gift is more generous than a loan—and besides, it would show the sister exactly how much confidence you have in her offer.

Ah yes, our Lord's teaching does run counter to the instincts of nature. Without his grace, we shouldn't merely be unable to carry them out—we shouldn't even understand them.

Reflection

Scripture tells us that we are created in the image and likeness of God. C.S. Lewis jumped to a logical conclusion, then, when he wrote: "Next to the Blessed Sacrament itself, your neighbor is the holiest object presented to your senses."

The fact is, we more often treat those around us as inconsequential than as holy. People can be irritating and mean-tempered and our instinctive reaction is to give as good as we get. Thérèse felt the same impulse but, clinging to the gospel, she returned good for evil.

Thérèse points out that love of neighbor is a matter of choice and the grace of God. The choice is up to us and Thérèse is confident that God will supply the grace. She doesn't say it will be easy but she insists that, if we are to follow the gospel, it is essential. "The command I give you is this, that you love one another" (Jn 15:17).

Prayer

Lord, nothing you ask me to do seems as difficult as loving my neighbor. Give me the strength not only to love when my neighbor is most unlovable, but to find joy in doing so. Prevent me from giving way to the impatience and anger that wounds others. Help me to act on the knowledge that we are all created in your image. Through Christ our Lord. Amen.

THREE

Embracing Suffering

Most people do their best to avoid suffering. Not Thérèse of Lisieux. In fact, she was so drawn to suffering that she said she felt it was a "magnet which drew me to itself.... I felt a deep, true love for it." "I thirsted for suffering," she said on one occasion and on another she stated that she wanted only one thing, "to suffer for Jesus always."

Readers who are enthusiastic over Thérèse's "little way" begin to have their doubts when they encounter material such as this. Ordinary life brings as much pain as most people can handle. Who needs a saint who thirsts for more?

Was Thérèse psychologically disturbed? Did she have a morbid interest in pain? In this regard, at any rate, she's not particularly appealing to contemporary society, caught up in the pursuit of happiness and material possessions.

On the other hand, perhaps Thérèse simply discovered and laid bare a truth implicit in the gospel: that suffering is redemptive and can draw us closer to God. This, in fact, is her point. She had as her model Jesus himself, the Suffering Servant who chose his Father's will above his own.

Thérèse had no interest in suffering for its own sake. She chose to embrace it for two reasons. First, she wanted God to know that her love for him was completely free of self-interest. In other words, she didn't love him for the blessings or consolations he might send her way but simply for himself.

In fact, he sent very few consolations to Thérèse. Her prayer life was barren, her daily life was one of continual sacrifice, and she endured tremendous spiritual and physical pain throughout the year before she died. She took it all in the manner of Job: "Slay me though he might, I will wait for him" (Job 13:15).

Second, and just as important, she offered up her suffering for the conversion of sinners. She noted that she wasn't called to Carmel for her own happiness. "I was to sacrifice my life for others and win heaven for sinners. As a mother of souls.... I would travail in sorrow."

In spite of the role suffering plays in Thérèse's spirituality, she was cautious about asking God to send some her way. "If I were to ask for sufferings," she said, "these would be mine and I would have to bear them alone and I've never been able to do anything alone."

As Thérèse matured, she actually focused less on suffering and more on conformity to God's will with whatever suffering that entailed.

Thérèse's approach to pain is simply the Christian approach, heightened by her ardent love for God and her intense desire to save souls. Further, the pain that Thérèse most often speaks of is the deep interior suffering that accompanies dying to self. This is nothing more than the cost of following the gospel. Embrace this, Thérèse says, and not only will you grow in holiness, but your suffering will serve as a prayer on behalf of sinners.

Martyrdom of the Heart: Interior Suffering

True courage does not consist in those momentary ardours which impel us to go out and win the world to Christ—at the cost of every imaginable danger, which only adds another touch of romance to our beautiful dreams.

No, the courage that counts with God is that type of courage which our Lord showed in the Garden of Olives: on the one hand, a natural desire to turn away from suffering; on the other, in anguish of soul the willing acceptance of the chalice which his Father had sent him.

In a letter to Céline, Thérèse provides a glimpse into the extent of her interior suffering. Her habitual lack of consolation in prayer and her sense of distance from God seem like martyrdom to her.

God is admirable, but he is especially lovable; let us love him, then... let us love him enough to suffer for him all that he wills, even spiritual pains, aridities, anxieties, apparent coldness....

Ah, here is great love, to love Jesus without feeling the sweetness of this love... this is martyrdom... unknown martyrdom, known to God alone, which the eye of the creature cannot discover, a martyrdom without honor, without triumph.... That is love pushed to the point of heroism....

But, one day, a grateful God will cry out: "Now, my turn." Oh, what will we see then?... What is this life which will no more have an end?... God will be the soul of our soul... unfathomable mystery....

The eye of man has not seen the uncreated light, his ear has not heard the incomparable harmonies, and his heart cannot have any idea of what God reserves for those whom he loves.

I have noticed that the experience of suffering makes us kind and indulgent toward others because it is suffering that draws us near to God.

... Trials help us detach ourselves from the earth; they make us look higher than this world. Here below nothing can satisfy us. One cannot enjoy a moment's rest save in constant readiness to do the will of God.

Shortly after Thérèse's First Communion, her sister Marie spoke to her about suffering. She told Thérèse that God would probably not allow her to suffer much but would carry her through life as a child. Thérèse thought about that and came to a different conclusion.

… I felt born within my heart a great desire to suffer, and at the same time the interior assurance that Jesus reserved a great number of crosses for me. I felt myself flooded with consolations so great that I look upon them as one of the greatest graces of my life.

Suffering became my attraction.… Up until this time, I had suffered without loving suffering, but since this day I felt a real love for it. I also felt the desire of loving only God, of finding my joy only in him.

Often during my Communions, I repeated these words of *The Imitation [of Christ]*: O Jesus, unspeakable sweetness, change all the consolations of this earth into bitterness for me."

If you want to secure any object, no matter what it is, you've got to find the right steps for attaining it.

And our Lord let me see clearly that if I wanted to win souls I'd got to do it by bearing a cross. So the more suffering came my way, the more strongly did suffering attract me.

My desire for suffering was answered, and yet my attraction for it did not diminish. My soul soon shared in the sufferings of my heart. Spiritual aridity was my daily bread and, deprived of all consolation, I was still the happiest of creatures....

I desire one thing only when I am in Carmel, and that is to suffer for Jesus always. Life passes so quickly that it is better to have a most splendid crown [in heaven] and a little suffering, than an ordinary crown and no suffering.

... I realise that one will love the good God better for all eternity, because of suffering borne with joy—! And, by suffering, one can save souls....

Sanctity lies not in saying beautiful things, or even in thinking them, or feeling them: it lies in truly being willing to suffer.

It is so sweet to serve our Lord in the night of trial; we have only this life to practice the virtue of faith.

I suffer much but do I suffer well? That is the important thing.

A Dark Night of the Soul

During the last year and a half of her life, Thérèse struggled with temptations to despair, unbelief, suicide, the fear that God didn't love her, that heaven didn't exist and that she was eternally damned.

This assault on her faith came unexpectedly and lasted until her death. Her suffering was extreme but she triumphed, making her an inspiring model for those who deal with similar doubts. The next excerpts are from this period of her life.

Jesus... allowed pitch-black darkness to sweep over my soul and let the thought of heaven, so sweet to me from infancy, destroy all my peace and torture me. This trial was not something lasting a few days or weeks. I suffered it for months and am still waiting for it to end.

I wish I could express what I feel but it is impossible. One must have travelled through the same sunless tunnel to understand how dark it is....

My sufferings increased whenever I grew wearied by the surrounding darkness and tried to find peace and strength by thinking of eternal life. For the voice of unbelievers came to mock me out of the darkness: "You dream of light, of a fragrant land, you dream that their Creator will be yours forever and you think you will one day leave behind this fog in which you languish. Hope on! Hope on!

And look forward to death! But it will give you, not what you hope for, but a still darker night, the night of annihilation."

... This story of my suffering is as inadequate as an artist's sketch compared with his model, but I do not want to write any more about it lest I should blaspheme. I am afraid I have already said too much.

May God forgive me! He knows very well that although I had not the consolation of faith, I forced myself to act as if I had. I have made more acts of faith in the last year than in the whole of my life.

Although Thérèse was troubled about the reality of heaven, she faced this dark night of the soul with courage and joy. Addressing herself to her mother superior, she explains how she met this spiritual assault.

I... take refuge in Jesus, telling him that I'm ready to defend the doctrine of heaven with the last drop of my blood. What does it matter, that I should catch no glimpse of its beauties, here on earth, if that will help poor sinners to see them in eternity?

And so, though it robs me of all enjoyment in life, this ordeal God has sent me, I can still tell him that everything he does is delightful to me; because after all there's no greater joy than to accept suffering for the love of him.

And if it's interior suffering, hidden away from

one's fellow creatures, he is all the better pleased. Although, for that matter, if he took no notice at all (supposing that were possible), it wouldn't worry me; I should still be glad to suffer if there were any chance of making reparation, in that way, for a single sin of unbelief.

... Does it sound as if I were exaggerating my symptoms? Of course, to judge by all the sentiments I express in all the nice little poems I've made up during the last year, you might imagine that my soul was as full of consolations as it could hold; that, for me, the veil which hides the unseen scarcely existed. And all the time it isn't just a veil, it's a great wall which reaches up to the sky and blots out the stars!

No, when I write poems about the happiness of heaven and the eternal possession of God, it strikes no chord of happiness in my own heart — I'm simply talking about what I'd determined to believe.

During the last year of her life, Thérèse was surprised by the extent of her physical and spiritual suffering. She didn't expect to suffer like this, she said, and her anguish and doubts are evident as she struggles to accept the challenge.

I wonder how God can hold himself back for such a long time from taking me. And then, one would say that he wants to make me believe that there is no heaven! And all the saints whom I love so much, where are they "hanging out"?

Ah! I'm not pretending, it's very true that I don't see a thing. But I must sing very strongly in my heart: "After death life is immortal," or without this, things would turn out badly.

The angels can't suffer; therefore, they are not as fortunate as I am. How astonished they would be if they suffered and felt what I feel! Yes, they'd be very surprised because so am I myself.

If you only knew what frightful thoughts obsess me! Pray very much for me in order that I do not listen to the devil who wants to persuade me about so many lies. It's the reasoning of the worst materialists which is imposed on my mind....

I want to do good after my death, but I will not be able to do so! It will be as it was for Mother Geneviève [the founder of the Lisieux Carmel]; We expected to see her work miracles, and complete silence fell over her tomb....

Must one have thoughts like this when one loves God so much!

Finally, I offer up these very great pains to obtain the light of faith for poor unbelievers, for all those who separate themselves from the church's beliefs.

Looking out her window, Thérèse pointed to a shady part of the garden and said:

… Down there, at the side of the chestnut trees, do you see that black hole wherein nothing is distinguishable?… Well I am in a place like that, as regards both body and soul…. Ah! yes, what darkness! But I dwell there in peace.

God gives me courage in proportion to my sufferings. I think at present I could not bear any more. But I am not afraid; for, if the sufferings increase, he will at the same time increase my courage.

Inner Conflict Caused by Aridity and Pain

Sometimes, when we are suffering, people ignore our pain and expect us to be cheerful or helpful. Thérèse had a similar experience. One of the sisters came into the infirmary every night, stood at the foot of Thérèse's bed, and smiled inanely at her. Here's how Thérèse handled this irritating behavior.

It is very painful to be the object of smiles when we are suffering, but I try to remember that Jesus on the cross underwent the same experience in the midst of his sufferings. Is it not said in the Gospel:

"They blasphemed him, wagging their heads." That thought helps me to offer up the sacrifice cheerfully.

In this letter to Céline, Thérèse reveals some of her conflicting thoughts regarding the aridity and pain that are her lot.

Life is often a burden; such bitterness, but such sweetness! Yes, life costs, it is hard beginning a day's work... if only one felt Jesus close at hand! Oh! One would do all for him... but no, he seems a thousand leagues away, we are alone with ourselves. Oh! How wearisome is company when Jesus is not there!

But what can that loving friend be doing? Doesn't he see our anguish, the weight that is crushing us? Where is he, why does he not come to console us, since we have no friend but him?

Alas!... He is not far off, he is here, close, looking at us, begging us to offer him this grief, this agony.... He needs it for souls [as an offering for sinners], for our soul. He means to give us so splendid a reward! His ambitions for us are so great.

But how will he say "My turn now" if we haven't had our turn, if we haven't given him a thing? Alas, it is great pain to him thus to fill our cup with sorrows, but he knows that is the only way to prepare us "to know him as he knows himself...."

Oh! What a destiny! How great a thing is our soul! Let us lift ourselves above all that passes, not stay close to earth. Higher, the air is pure! Jesus is hidden but one senses him....

This morning I read a passage in the Gospel where it is said: "I am come not to bring peace but a sword." All that remains for us then is to fight. When we have not the strength, it is then that Jesus fights for us.

Weary but Unwavering

Thérèse's weariness coupled with her determination are evident in this letter to Céline.

This evening I felt a need... to forget the earth. Here below, everything wearies me, everything is an effort. I find only one joy, to suffer for Jesus....

Life passes... eternity comes to meet us with great strides. Soon we shall be living with the very life of Jesus. Having drunk deep at the source of all bitterness, we shall be deified [become one with Jesus] in the very source of all joys, of all delights....

"The fashion of this world passes away" [1 Cor 7:31]... soon we shall see new heavens. Immensity will be our abode. We shall be no more prisoners on this earth of our exile, all will have passed away! With our heavenly spouse, we shall skim over lakes with no shore.... "Courage, Jesus hears our sorrow, even to its last echo."

"Now our harps are hung up on the willows by the river of Babylon" [Ps 86:2], but on the day of our deliverance, what harmonies shall we not draw from them! With what joy shall we set all the strings of our instruments vibrating!

Let us offer our sufferings to Jesus to save souls. Poor souls... they have fewer graces than we, yet all the blood of a God has been shed to save them. Jesus has chosen to make their salvation depend on a sigh of our heart. [In other words, she must intercede and offer her sufferings for the conversion of sinners.]

What a mystery is there. If a sigh can save a soul, what cannot sufferings like ours do? Let us refuse Jesus nothing!

Peace in Suffering

In this letter to Céline, Thérèse reflects on how to suffer in peace.

We must see life in its true light.... It is an instant between two eternities. Let us suffer in peace!

I admit that the word peace struck me as rather strong, but the other day, thinking it over, I hit upon the secret of suffering in peace. The word peace does not mean joy, at least not felt joy. To suffer in peace it is enough to will whatever Jesus wills.

It helps so much, when one is suffering, to have loving hearts to echo back our grief.

Prudent and Never Despairing

In spite of her love for suffering, Thérèse was prudent about how she prayed for it. She was careful not to go beyond what God himself had for her.

I would never ask God for greater sufferings for then they would be my own sufferings and I should have to bear them all alone, and I have never been able to do anything of myself.

Thérèse never allowed her suffering to take the form of melancholy or depression over her shortcomings. When Pauline confided that she felt sad and discouraged over her faults,
Thérèse responded in her practical, upbeat way.

… As for me, I never allow myself to be discouraged. When I commit a fault that makes me sad, I know well the sadness is a consequence of my un-faithfulness. But do you think that I rest there? Oh, no! Straightway, I hasten to say to God: My God, I know that I have deserved this feeling of sadness I experience. Meanwhile, let me offer it to you all the same as an ordeal you have sent me—through love. I am sorry for what I have done, but I am glad to have this suffering to offer to you.

We who run in the way of love shouldn't be thinking of sufferings that can take place in the future. It's a lack of confidence, it's like meddling in the work of creation.

Reflection

Many Christians today claim that God automatically blesses believers with prosperity and freedom from pain. Thérèse would vigorously refute this, pointing to the example of Jesus himself.

Not all suffering should be endured, of course. Emotional and physical pain that can be eased should be eased. Beyond that, however, life is full of difficulty. We can ignore it or avoid it, or we can profit from it.

As St. Francis of Assisi said when speaking of suffering: "If this was God's life on earth, what choice have I but to make it my own?"

Prayer

Lord, help me to accept the suffering that comes my way. I want to overcome my fear and, through my pain, I want to draw closer to you. In the dark night of my suffering, you alone are my light. Through Christ our Lord. Amen.

FOUR

The Little Way

NOT TOO LONG AGO, Mother Teresa established a house for her Sisters of Charity in a run-down neighborhood in Washington, D.C. The press was on hand when she arrived to help her sisters settle in and one reporter asked what she hoped to accomplish there.

"The joy of loving and being loved," she replied. "That takes a lot of money, doesn't it?," another reporter asked. "No," Mother Teresa answered, "It takes a lot of sacrifice."

One hundred years earlier, Thérèse of Lisieux hit upon the same answer to many of life's problems: sacrifice. Money and social position were not the answer, Thérèse decided, but countless small sacrifices offered to God might count for much.

This sort of hidden, quiet life didn't automatically appeal to Thérèse. Actually, she longed for a heroic life in which she could die as a martyr or spend herself as a missionary. But she lacked the stamina and opportunity for a rigorous, public ministry and so she sought a more realistic path to God.

This turned out to be her "little way of spiritual childhood," characterized by humility and childlike confidence in God. It's an approach available to anyone, anytime, anywhere, and requires only the will to serve God and others in small, everyday ways.

Personal need drove Thérèse to develop her "little way." She wanted to be a saint but felt that she was too "little," that she didn't measure up to the high standards set by the saints. She concluded that God himself would lift her to the heights of sanctity if she would rely on him as a child relies on her parents.

The "little way" often found expression in small sacrifices and acts of kindness done in secret. When doing the laundry in the heat of summer, for example, Thérèse chose the hottest place in the room, leaving the cooler places to the other nuns. Thérèse suffered intensely from the frigid winter weather in the unheated convent. She never complained, however, and it wasn't until she was on her deathbed that she revealed that some winters she thought she would die of the cold.

Thérèse's "little way" couldn't be simpler or more easy to adopt. It encompasses all the virtues such as humility, love of neighbor, and trust in God but it doesn't require a complicated scheme to carry it off. All that's necessary is the desire to put God and others first, ourselves second.

For Thérèse, the "little way" was her response to the invasion of her heart by Jesus. His love for her overwhelmed her. She, in turn, "wanted to love Jesus passionately"... to "give him a thousand marks of love, as long as I was able to do so." She did this dozens of times a day through the most mundane sacrifices and kindnesses.

It worked. Her life may have been hidden and her sacrifices small, but they earned her a place in heaven and the honor of the church.

Smallness before the Lord

I care now about one thing only—to love you, my Jesus! Great deeds are forbidden me, I cannot preach the gospel nor shed my blood—but what does it matter? [Missionaries and priests] toil instead of me and I, a little child, well, I keep close to the throne of God and I love for those who fight.

Love proves itself by deeds, so how am I to show my love? Well, I will scatter flowers, perfuming the divine throne with their fragrance, and I'll sweetly sing my hymn of love. Yes, my beloved, that is how I'll spend my short life.

The only way I can prove my love is by scattering flowers and those flowers are every little sacrifice, every glance and word, and the doing of the least of actions for love. I wish both to suffer and to find joy through love.

Thérèse felt that she didn't have what it takes to be a saint. She was too inconsequential—too small—to achieve great sanctity. One day, the Lord revealed to her that he honored her littleness, and in fact, wanted her to remain that way. He himself would provide the way for Thérèse—and all those who have a simple trust in him—to reach heaven.

I have always wanted to become a saint. Unfortunately, when I have compared myself to the saints, I have always found that there is the same distance between the saints and me as there is between a mountain whose summit is lost in the clouds and a humble grain of sand trodden underfoot by passers-by.

Instead of being discouraged, I told myself: God would not make me wish for something impossible and so, in spite of my littleness, I can aim at being a saint. It is impossible for me to grow bigger, so I put up with myself as I am, with all my countless faults. But I will look for some means of going to heaven by a little way which is very short and very straight, a little way that is quite new.

We live in an age of inventions. We need no longer climb laboriously up flights of stairs; in well-to-do houses there are lifts [elevators]. And I was determined to find a lift to carry me to Jesus, for I was far too small to climb the steep stairs of perfection.

So I sought in holy Scripture some idea of what this lift I wanted would be, and I read these words from the very mouth of eternal wisdom: "Whosoever is a little one, let him come to me." I drew nearer to God, fully realising that I had found what I was looking for.

I also wanted to know how God would deal with a "little one," so I continued my search and found this: "You shall be carried at the breasts and on the knees; as one whom the mother caresseth, so will I comfort you."

It is your arms, Jesus, which are the lift to carry me to heaven.

A Hidden Life of Sacrifice

With astonishing confidence, Thérèse declared on several occasions that she would be a saint. She would achieve that distinction through her hidden, silent life of sacrifice.

God made me realise that the true glory is that which is eternal and that, to achieve it, there is no need to perform outstanding deeds. Instead, one must remain hidden and perform one's good deeds so that the right hand knows not what the left hand does.

When I read stories about the deeds of the great French heroines—especially of [St.] Joan of Arc—I longed to imitate them and felt stirred by the same inspiration which moved them.

It was then that I received one of the greatest graces of my life.... I was made to understand that the glory I was to win would never be seen during my lifetime. My glory would consist in becoming a great saint!

This desire might seem presumptuous, seeing how weak and imperfect I was and still am, even after eight years as a nun, yet I always feel the same fearless certainty that I shall become a great saint.

I'm not relying on my own merits, as I have none, but I put my hope in him who is goodness and holiness himself. It is he alone who, satisfied with my feeble efforts, will raise me to him, will clothe me with his infinite merits, and will make me a saint. I did not realise then how much one had to suffer to be a saint, but God soon showed me this....

Thérèse had hoped to enter Carmel before Lent of 1888. For various reasons, however, she was denied admission until after Easter. She was tempted to relax her strict preparations for the convent but decided, instead, to continue her mortifications. True to her "little way," these penances were very simple and ordinary.

How did I pass those three months, a time, as it proved, so full of graces? My first thought was that perhaps I'd better give up living by a rather strict rule as my habit had been of late. After all, why worry about that now?

But before long I came to realise that this respite was a precious opportunity, and decided to give myself up, more than ever, to a recollected and mortified way of life.

When I say "mortified," I don't mean to suggest that I went in for penitential practices of any kind. That's a thing, I'm afraid, I've never done. I've heard so much about saintly people who took on the most rigorous mortifications from their childhood upwards, but I'd never tried to imitate them—the idea never had any attractions for me.

Instead of that, I'd allowed people to wrap me up in cotton wool, to treat me like a bird that's being fattened for market, as if there were no need for penance in my life at all.

What I did try to do by way of mortification was to thwart my self-will, which always seemed determined to get its own way; to repress the re-joinder which sometimes came to my lips; to do little acts of kindness without attaching any impor-tance to them; to sit upright instead of leaning back in my chair.

That wasn't much, was it? But I did make these

insignificant efforts to make myself less unworthy of a heavenly bridegroom.

The War against Myself

Thérèse had neither the opportunity nor, as she matured, the inclination to perform rigorous penances. Her life in the convent was extremely ascetical, but beyond that she viewed penance from the perspective of her "little way." In the next two excerpts, she comments on the penitential practices of the saints.

Our Lord assured us that in our Father's house there are many mansions.... If every soul called to perfection were obliged to perform... austerities in order to enter heaven, our Lord would have given us some clear indication of it and we would respond eagerly. But he himself has declared, "In my Father's house there are many mansions."

If, then, there are mansions set apart for great souls, for the Fathers of the desert and for the martyrs of penance, there must also be one for little children. So a place is waiting for us there if we but love him dearly together with our heavenly Father and the Spirit of Love.

In the life of Blessed Henry Suso there is a very striking passage with regard to corporal penances.

He had undertaken the most frightful penances,

which had well-nigh ruined his health, when an angel appeared to him and told him to stop, adding: "You are not to fight any longer as a simple soldier. From this moment, I shall arm you as a knight." And he made the saint understand the superiority of the spiritual conflict over the mortifications of the flesh.

Very well… God has not willed me to fight as a simple soldier. He armed me at once as a knight, and I have engaged in the war against myself in the spiritual domain by abnegation and little hidden sacrifices.

I have found peace and humility in that hidden conflict wherein nature finds nothing for herself.

Above all, I tried to do my small good deeds in secret. I loved folding up the mantles forgotten by the sisters and seized every possible opportunity of helping them. I was also attracted towards penance, but I was not allowed to satisfy my longing.

The only mortification granted me was to master my self-love, and that did me far more good than any bodily penance.

Small Sacrifices and the Virtue of Detachment

It's not easy to act on the small sacrificial opportunities that come our way every day. Thérèse offers a suggestion for overcoming our reluctance.

How many souls plead: "I have not enough forti-
tude to accomplish such an act [of sacrifice]." But let
them put forth some effort! The good God never
refuses the first grace which imparts courage to act.
After that, the heart is strengthened and the soul
goes on from victory to victory.

Thérèse's "little way" includes the virtue of detach-
ment. Here, she gives a fellow nun advice on how she
ought to approach her work.

Keep yourself interiorly detached and free from
any piece of work you might be doing. Always let
the nuns give you advice and suggestions about it
and do not object if they touch it up, even in your
absence.

Naturally, because of differences of taste, they
might, in this way, spoil it and you will begin to
count as wasted the hours you have devoted to it....

The goal of all our undertakings should not be
so much a task perfectly completed but the accomplishment of the will of God.

When I am feeling nothing, when I am incapable of
praying, of practicing virtue, then is the moment for
seeking opportunities, nothings, which please Jesus
more than mastery of the world or even martyrdom suffered with generosity. For example, a

smile, a friendly word when I would want to say nothing, or put on a look of annoyance....

Experience taught me that the only way to get happiness in this world is to hide oneself away and remain in ignorance of all created things. I know that without love all we do is worthless.

It is the little crosses that are our whole joy. They are more common than big ones and prepare the heart to receive the latter when this is the will of our good Master.

Reflection

Thérèse lived life on the edge. Entering the convent was something like entering the spiritual equivalent of the Olympics. The nuns weren't in competition with each other, of course, but their training pushed them to achieve their personal best. They learned to endure suffering and practice self-denial in the pursuit of their goal.

Flannery O'Connor, the novelist, once said, "It is the extreme situation that best reveals what we are essentially." Thérèse was essentially a lover of God and his people. Her "little way" pushed her into the extremes of sacrifice and there her holiness was revealed.

Prayer

Lord, the opportunities for holiness are all around me. Every day I miss many chances to serve others in little ways and to offer small sacrifices to you. Help me to seize the moment, confident that you will give me the grace to triumph over my own laziness and reluctance to serve. Through Christ our Lord. Amen.

FIVE

Humility:
Nothing to Give,
but Giving It All

Most of Thérèse's fellow nuns regarded her as a good nun, even an exceptional nun, but nothing more—certainly not a saint. Her sister Céline summed up the general feeling when she said, "One never noticed anything extraordinary about her."

There is a famous story regarding Thérèse and the obituary notice that Carmelite convents customarily sent to one another on the death of one of their own. One of the sisters was speculating on what the mother prioress could possibly find to say about Thérèse. "Though she is very good," the sister said dismissively, "she has never done anything worth talking about."

Nothing could have pleased Thérèse more, except not to have been noticed at all. She wanted to be "trod under foot like a grain of sand," she said, "… to be forgotten… not only by creatures but by myself."

Thérèse wasn't suffering from a massive case of low self-esteem, as these statements might indicate. On the contrary, Thérèse had an extremely healthy ego. God had created her and he had redeemed her. Not for a moment did she doubt her self-worth.

The point of Thérèse's humility was simply to clear the ground so that Jesus alone could live within her. This "littleness" allowed her to see herself as she really was—imperfect and dependent on God—but freed her from an excessive preoccupation with her own shortcomings. "We have merely to love him," she said, "without examining our faults too closely."

Thérèse never gave in to false modesty or self-pity, two traits commonly mistaken for humility. Nor was she passive. She may have been weak and little, as she said, but she wasn't helpless. She pursued humility with an almost frightening intensity. It was, in fact, the basis for her "little way."

"The glory of my Jesus," she said. "That is all." By vigorously emptying herself for him, she hoped to imitate and attract him who had emptied himself for her.

Humbleness of Heart

… Never seek what seems great in the eyes of creatures. Solomon, the wisest king there was upon the earth, having considered all the various labors that occupy men under the sun—painting, sculpture, all the arts—realised that all these things were subject to envy and cried out that they are nought but "vanity and affliction of spirit."

The one thing that is not envied is the last place; the last place is the one thing that is not vanity and affliction of spirit.

In a letter to Céline, Thérèse urges her sister to remain humble and faithful to God in small things.

… [Jesus] is glad that you feel your weakness; it is he who imprints upon your soul its feeling of self-distrust. Thank Jesus…. If you always stay faithful to pleasing him in small things, he will be under obligation to aid you in great.

Without our Lord, the apostles labored all night and caught no fish, but their labor was pleasing to Jesus. He wanted to prove to them that he alone can give us anything. He wanted the apostles to be humbled….

"Sons," he said to them, "have you nothing to eat?" "Lord," answered Peter, "we have fished all night and taken nothing." Maybe, if he had caught a few small fish, Jesus would not have worked a miracle, but he had nothing, so Jesus soon filled his net so that it almost broke.

There you have Jesus' character: as God he gives, but he requires humbleness of heart.

What a happiness it is to be humbled! It is the one way that makes saints!

Whenever you are lacking in virtue, you should not excuse yourself by throwing the blame on physical causes, on the weather, or some other trial. Instead, you should make it a means of self-humiliation and then go to take your place in the rank and file of little souls, since you are so weak in the practice of virtue.

Your soul's urgent need at present is not the ability to practice heroic virtue but rather to acquire humility.

Alas! When I remember my days as a novice, I see how imperfect I was. I laugh now at some of the things I did.... In the days to come it may be that my present state will seem most imperfect, but I am no longer surprised by anything and I feel no distress at seeing my complete helplessness.

On the contrary, I glory in it and every day I expect to discover fresh flaws in myself. In fact, this revelation of my nothingness does me much more good than being enlightened on matters of faith.

Devotion to the Holy Face

Thérèse's full name as a religious was Thérèse of the Child Jesus and the Holy Face. "The Holy Face" is a reference to the face of Jesus disfigured by suffering as described in Isaiah 52. The total humility depicted there motivated her spiritual life.

My devotion to the Holy Face, or rather all my spirituality, has been based on these words of Isaiah: "There is no beauty in him, nor comeliness: and we have seen him, and there was no sightliness [in him].... Despised and the most abject of men, a man of sorrows and acquainted with infirmity: and his look is as it were hidden and despised, whereupon we esteemed him not."

I, too, desire to be without glory or beauty, to tread the winepress alone, unknown to any creature.

Pauline first introduced Thérèse to the devotion of the Holy Face. Here she reminds Pauline of that and reveals the impact this devotion has had on her spirituality.

... I had known nothing of the richness of the treasures of the Holy Face and it was you who made me acquainted with them. Just as you were the first of us to enter Carmel, so you were the first to explore the mysteries of love hidden in the face of Jesus. You revealed them to me and I understood more clearly than ever what true glory is.

He whose kingdom is not of this world showed me that the only condition worth coveting is "to want to be ignored and regarded as nothing, to find joy in contempt of self."

I wanted my face, like the face of Jesus, to be, as it were, hidden and unrecognised.

Holiness does not consist in this or that practice. It consists in a disposition of the heart, which makes us always humble and little in the arms of God, well aware of our feebleness, but boldly confident in the Father's goodness.

True Nobility

Mr. Martin, Thérèse, and Céline went on a pilgrimage to Rome shortly before Thérèse entered Carmel. The wealth and social position of the others on the trip prompted Thérèse to reflect on true nobility.

The pilgrimage was made up almost entirely of people of birth and position. It was the first time Céline and I had found ourselves among such people. But we weren't dazzled by them, for all their titles seemed quite empty and meaningless.

I understood those words of *The Imitation [of Christ]*: "Be not solicitous for the shadow of a great name." I understood that true greatness has nothing to do with a title. It's a matter of the soul.

The prophet Isaiah says that God "will have a new name for his own servants," and in St. John we read that to the victor God will give "a white stone, on which stone a new name is written, known to him only who receives it."

It is in heaven that we shall know our titles of nobility. Then "each of us will receive his due award from God." The first, the most noble, and the richest will be he who on earth chose to be the poorest and least known for love of our Lord.

In the early days of my own spiritual life, when I was about thirteen or fourteen, I used to wonder what further heights there could still be for me to climb. I didn't see how I could possibly get a clearer idea of what perfection meant.

But, of course, I realised before long that the further you go along that road, the more conscious you are of the distance between you and the goal, and by now–well, by now I'm resigned to seeing myself always far from perfect; even glad, in a way, to see how much more there is to do.

God has need of no one, so let us not take foolish pride in the thought that he decides to make use of us at times.

We should… attribute nothing of good to ourselves. No one actually possesses the virtues he practices, so let everything redound to the glory of God.

A Share in Jesus' Humiliation

On her pilgrimage to Rome, Thérèse noticed that there were greater restrictions placed on women than on men. Women, for example, were not allowed in certain parts of shrines or churches. She saw this as an opportunity to share in Jesus' humiliation but left the matter open, to be settled in heaven.

There's no respect for us poor wretched women anywhere. And yet you'll find the love of God much commoner among women than among men, and the women at the crucifixion showed much more courage than the apostles, exposing themselves to insult and wiping our Lord's face.

I suppose he lets us share the neglect he himself chose for his lot on earth. In heaven, where the last will be first, we shall know more about what God thinks.

… My life has been a happy one because I have tried to put self-seeking away from me. The only way to attain happiness is to know perfect love.

And the only way to attain perfect love is to forget self entirely and never to seek gratification in anything.

Those who judge you unfavorably are not robbing you of anything. You are none the poorer for all they may say. It is they who are really the losers.... Is there anything sweeter than the inward joy that comes from thinking well of others!

If, for the love of God, you truly humble yourself when judged unfavorably by others, it is all the better for you and all the worse for your critics.

Reliance on God

Thérèse stressed the importance of relying on God's strength, not our own. Had St. Peter done so, he would never have endured the humiliation of denying Jesus before the crucifixion.

Consider the example of little children. They are always breaking things, tearing their clothes, or falling down and all the while they are loving their parents very much. And so when I fall, like a little child, it makes me lay the finger on my nothingness and my weakness, and I think to myself: "What would happen to me, to what lengths would I go, were I to depend on my own strength?"

I can well understand how St. Peter fell. Poor St. Peter! He relied on self instead of leaning on the power of God. I am sure if he had said humbly to Jesus: "I beseech you to give me the courage to follow you even unto death," that courage would have been granted him instantly.

Furthermore, I am certain, too, our Lord taught no more to his apostles by his instructions and by his visible presence than he teaches to us by the inspirations of his grace.

He could have said to Peter: "Ask me for the strength to accomplish what you desire to do." But no, since he destined Peter to govern the whole church, in which there are many sinners, he willed that he should experience in himself just what man is without the grace of God.

It was for this reason that Jesus said to him before his fall: "And you, being once converted, confirm your brethren." In other words, tell them the story of your fall. Show them—by describing your own experience—the disastrous effects of resting on human props.

Better Not to Fight

Thérèse's humility was such that she would admit she was not always able to respond to a difficult situation with love. When that was the case, she simply fled. Here, she gives an example not only of this stratagem but of her own imperfection and humble willingness to see herself as she was. She is speaking to her mother superior.

I have… told you, Mother, of my last resolve for avoiding a defeat in the struggles of life—desertion. I used this rather dishonorable trick when I was a novice and it was always completely successful. I will give you a striking example which, I think, will make you smile.

You had been ill for some days with bronchitis and we were very worried. One morning I came… to the infirmary to put back the keys of the Communion grill for I was sacristan. I was feeling delighted at having this opportunity of seeing you, but I took good care not to let it be seen.

One of the sisters, full of zeal, thought I was going to waken you and tried to take the keys quietly from me. I told her, as politely as possible, that I was just as eager as she was to make no noise, and added that it was my duty to return the keys…. I… tried to push my way into the room in spite of her. Then, what we feared, happened. The noise we made woke you and all the blame fell on me! The sister I had opposed hastened to make quite a speech, the gist of which was: "It was Sister Thérèse of the Child Jesus who made the noise."…

I burned to defend myself but fortunately I had a bright idea. I knew… that if I began to speak up for myself I should lose my peace of soul… my only hope of safety was to run away.

No sooner thought than done: I fled.… It was undoubtedly a queer kind of courage, but I think it is better not to fight when defeat is certain.

Opportunities to Grow in Humility

Although she was never officially appointed to the office, Thérèse served as the mistress of novices. The novices heaped praise on her, which distressed Thérèse. Since she always allowed them to speak freely to her, however, occasionally one of them would criticize her severely. Thérèse accepted such reprimands as an opportunity to grow in humility.

… I sometimes get a terrible longing to hear something said about me which isn't praise!… When that happens, our Lord arranges for somebody to give me what I call a nice little salad. Plenty of vinegar, plenty of spice about it. Nothing left out except the oil, and that makes it all the more tasty.

These nice little salads are served up to me by the novices when I least expect it. God lifts the veil that hides my imperfections, and these dear young sisters of mine see me just as I am. They don't care for that very much.

They tell me, with delightful frankness, all about the rough time I give them, and my unpleasant habits, with so little embarrassment that you would imagine they were talking about somebody else. You see, they know they are giving me an enormous amount of pleasure by doing it....

One day, when I was particularly anxious to be humiliated like that, one of the novices carried out my wishes so conscientiously that it reminded me, all at once, of Semei cursing King David [2 Sm 16:11]. "Yes," I said to myself, "sure enough, she must have had her orders from heaven to talk to me like that." No stint, there, of well-seasoned food in which my soul took an epicure's delight!

That's the sort of way in which God, mercifully, keeps me going. He can't be always supplying me with the food that really gives me strength—I mean, public humiliation of this kind—but every now and then there are crumbs falling from the... table to sustain me.

Jesus, Our Model of Humility

Jesus himself was the model for Thérèse's humility. He leaves himself vulnerable to us, in a manner of speaking, waiting for but never demanding our love.

… How small were the number of our Lord's friends when he was silent before his judges!… Oh, what a melody for my heart is that silence of Jesus. … He makes himself poor that we may be able to do him charity.

He stretches out his hand to us like a beggar, that on the sunlit day of judgement, when he appears in his glory, he may be able to utter and we to hear the loving words: "Come, blessed of my father; for I was hungry and you gave me to eat; I was thirsty and you gave me to drink; I was a stranger and you took me in; I was in prison, sick and you came to me."

It was Jesus himself who uttered those words, it is he who wants our love, begs for it. He puts himself, so to say, at our mercy. He wills to take nothing unless we give it to him and the smallest thing is precious in his divine eyes.…

We must be like Jesus, like Jesus whose look was hidden. [Is 52:3]… "Do you want to learn something that may serve you?" says *The Imitation [of Christ]*. "Love to be ignored and accounted for nothing." And in another place: "After you have left everything, you must above all leave yourself."

In a letter to her cousin, Marie Guerin, Thérèse revealed more of her understanding of humility.

... If you are nothing, you must not forget Jesus is all, so you must lose your little nothing in his infinite all and from now on think only of that uniquely lovable all....

Nor must you desire to see the fruits of your efforts. Jesus likes to keep for himself alone, these little nothings which console him....

You are wrong if you think your little Thérèse always marches with ardour along the way of virtue. She is weak, very weak. Every day she experiences it afresh. But... Jesus delights to teach her, as he taught St. Paul, the science of glorying in one's infirmities [2 Cor 12:5].

That is a great peace and I beg Jesus to teach it to you, for in it alone is found peace and rest for the heart.

As a Grain of Sand

The things of the world had no interest for Thérèse. She understood God's love so completely that she wanted nothing to stand in the way of receiving him. Here she speaks of herself in the third person, as a grain of sand.

... It [the grain of sand] desires to be reduced to nothing, unknown by any creature.... It desires nothing more, nothing but to be forgotten....

Yes, I want to be forgotten, and not only by creatures but also by myself. I should like to be so reduced to nothingness as to have no desire left....

The glory of my Jesus, that is all! For my own, I abandon it to him and if he seems to forget me, very well, he is free to since I am no longer mine but his....

He will weary of keeping me waiting sooner than I of waiting for him!

Intellect Subject to Humility

A person possessing intellectual gifts and spiritual insights can easily succumb to arrogance. Blessed with abundant wisdom, Thérèse herself found it difficult to avoid a sense of pride in her ability. Eventually, she realized that the intellect is as subject to humility as any other aspect of the personality.

... There are certain movements of the mind and heart, certain deep-reaching thoughts, that go to form a treasury of your very own. Nobody else, you feel, has a right to tamper with it.

For instance, I tell one of the sisters, when we have leave to talk, about some light that has been given to me in prayer; and she, quite soon after-wards, mentions it to a third party in conversation as if it were an idea of her own. Isn't that pilfering?

Or again, in recreation, I whisper some remark to the person next to me, a good remark, abso-lutely to the point and she repeats it aloud without mentioning where it came from. Isn't that a theft of my property? I can't say so at the time but I'd like to…. If opportunity arises, I determine to let it be known, with all the delicacy in the world, that some-body's been misappropriating my thoughts….

I really think I can say now that our Lord's given me the grace to care as little about gifts of the mind and the heart as about worldly possessions. An idea occurs to me and I say something which is well-received by the other sisters—why shouldn't they adopt it as their own? I find it quite natural.

You see, this idea doesn't belong to me, it be-longs to the Holy Spirit. Doesn't St. Paul tell us that we can't even say "Father" to our Father in heaven without the aid of his loving Spirit? Surely, then, he can make use of me if he wants to convey to any soul some profitable thought?

To suppose that this "thought" belongs to me would be to make the same mistake as the donkey carrying the relics, which imagined that all the rev-erence shown to the saints was meant for its own benefit!

Reflection

John Vianney, the Curé of Ars, had tremendous spiritual insights and spectacular success in bringing people to the Lord. Of his extraordinary ministry he simply said: "I have been privileged to give great gifts from my empty hands."

In his unassuming way, the Curé captured much of Thérèse's thinking on humility. Both would agree on the importance of this virtue. Both practiced it so intensely that it produced great sanctity. Thérèse urged all those interested in holiness to embrace it.

Certainly it is one of the most appealing, if least practiced, virtues. If we make it ours, we, too, will find that the Lord will give the greatest gift—himself—through our empty hands.

Prayer

How humble you were, Lord, to come to earth in the form of a man. Free me from the pride that prevents me from imitating your humility. Help me to see that the greatest person is the one who quietly serves the needs of others. Through Christ our Lord. Amen.

SIX

Difficulties in Prayer

Aᴛ ᴛʜᴇ ᴍɪɴɪᴍᴜᴍ, most of us expect saints to stay awake when they pray. Of course, we expect much more than that—revelations and ecstasies, for example—but at the very least we assume they'll remain alert. In a striking departure from tradition, Thérèse slept—not always but often enough.

Although she loved prayer, she grew distracted, found group prayer difficult, and experienced tremendous spiritual aridity. Her sister Céline said that she didn't think a soul ever received less consolation in prayer than Thérèse.

At last, a saint with whom most people can identify! True to her "little way," Thérèse once said that she wanted there to be nothing about her that other people might envy. This extended to her prayer life. The more ordinary that was, the more readily people could identify with it.

During her seven years in the convent, Thérèse did receive occasional consolations in prayer but these were extremely rare and virtually ceased toward the end. "Extraordinary mystical phenomena in her life were quite exceptional," her sister Pauline said. "Simplicity was the rule." Thérèse herself said: "I know of no ecstasy to which I do not prefer sacrifice. There I find happiness and there alone."

In spite of the difficulties, Thérèse remained faithful to prayer and relished her time with the Lord. She was there to love and comfort him, demanding no comfort in return. The fact that she received none is meant to encourage rather than discourage us.

Her prayer life underlines the point that holiness doesn't rest on warm feelings, visions, and prophecies but on the attitude of the heart before God.

Spiritual Dryness in Prayer

In her autobiography, Thérèse explains how she handled the spiritual dryness that plagued her. She focuses on the retreat she attended before taking her vows as a Carmelite.

Now I'll tell you of the retreat before my Profession. I was far from getting any consolation from it. Instead, I suffered complete spiritual dryness, almost as if I were quite forsaken.

As usual, Jesus slept in my little boat.... It's likely that as far as I'm concerned, he will stay asleep until the great final retreat of eternity. But that doesn't upset me. It fills me with great joy.

It's true that I'm a long way from being a saint, and this attitude of mine proves it. Instead of delighting in my spiritual aridity, I ought to blame my lack of faith and fervor for it. I should be distressed that I drop off to sleep during my prayers and during my thanksgiving after Holy Communion. But I don't feel at all distressed.

I know that children are just as dear to their parents whether they are asleep or awake and I know that doctors put their patients to sleep before they operate. So I just think that God "knoweth our frame. He remembereth that we are dust."

I can't say that I frequently received consolations when making my thanksgivings after Mass; perhaps it is the time when I receive the least. However, I find this very understandable since I have offered myself to Jesus not as one desirous of her own consolation in his visit but simply to please him who is giving himself to me.

When I am preparing for Holy Communion, I picture my soul as a piece of land and I beg the Blessed Virgin to remove from it any rubbish that would prevent it from being free; then I ask her to set up a huge tent worthy of heaven, adorning it with her own jewelry; finally, I invite all the angels and saints to come and conduct a magnificent concert there. It seems to me that when Jesus descends into my heart he is content to find himself so well received and I, too, am content.

All this, however, does not prevent both distractions and sleepiness from visiting me, but at the end of the thanksgiving, when I see that I have made it so badly, I make a resolution to be thankful all the rest of the day.

Archimedes said: "Give me a fulcrum and with a lever I will move the world." What he could not get, the saints have been given. The Almighty has given them a fulcrum: himself, himself alone. For a lever they have that prayer which burns with the fire of love.

Thus they have moved the world, and it with this lever that those still battling in the world move it and will go on moving it till the end of time.

All my strength lies in prayer and sacrifice. They are my invincible weapons, and I know, by experience, that they can soften the heart much better than words.

Talking to God... is always better than talking about God; those pious conversations—there's always a touch of self-approval about them.

... Saying the rosary takes it out of me more than any hair-shirt would; I do say it so badly! Try as I will to put force on myself, I can't meditate on the mysteries of the rosary; I just can't fix my mind on them.

For a long time I was in despair about it, this want of devotion. I couldn't understand it, because I've such a love for the Blessed Virgin that there ought to be no difficulty about saying prayers in her honor; her own favorite prayers, too!

Now I don't distress myself so much; it seems to me that the Queen of heaven, being my mother, must be aware of my good intentions, and that's enough for her.

Sometimes, when I'm in such a state of spiritual dryness that I can't find a single thought in my mind which will bring me close to God, I say an Our Father and a Hail Mary very slowly indeed. How they take me out of myself then; what solid satisfaction they give me then! Much more than if I'd hurried through them a hundred times over.

Meanwhile, the Blessed Virgin isn't angry with me; she shows that by always coming to my rescue the moment I ask her to. Any anxiety, any difficulty, makes me turn to her at once, and you couldn't have a more loving mother to see you through.

How many lights have I not drawn from the works of our holy father, St. John of the Cross! At the ages of seventeen and eighteen I had no other spiritual nourishment; later on, however, all books left me in aridity and I'm still in that state.

If I open a book by a spiritual author (even the most beautiful, the most touching book), I feel my heart contract immediately and I read without understanding, so to speak. Or if I do understand, my mind comes to a standstill without the capacity of meditating. In this helplessness, Holy Scripture and *The Imitation [of Christ]* come to my aid; in them I discover a solid and very pure nourishment.

But it is especially the Gospels which sustain me during my hours of prayer, for in them I find what is necessary for my poor little soul. I am constantly discovering in them new lights, hidden and mysterious meanings.

I understand and I know from experience that: "The kingdom of God is within you".... Never have I heard [Jesus] speak, but I feel that he is within me at each moment; he is guiding and inspiring me with what I must say and do.

I find just when I need them certain lights which I had not seen until then, and it isn't most frequently during my hours of prayer that these are most abundant but rather in the midst of my daily occupations.

The Power of Prayer

The power of prayer is really tremendous. It makes one like a queen who can approach the king at any time and get whatever she asks for. To be sure of an answer, there is no need to recite from a book a formula composed for the occasion. If there were, I should have to be pitied.

Though I'm quite unworthy, I love to say the Divine Office every day, but apart from that I cannot bring myself to hunt through books for beautiful prayers. There are so many of them that I get a headache. Besides, each prayer seems lovelier than the next. I cannot possibly say them all and do not know which to choose. I behave like children who cannot read: I tell God very simply what I want and he always understands.

For me, prayer is an upward leap of the heart, an untroubled glance towards heaven, a cry of gratitude and love which I utter from the depths of sorrow as well as from the heights of joy. It has a supernatural grandeur which expands the soul and unites it with God.

I say an Our Father or a Hail Mary when I feel

so spiritually barren that I cannot summon up a single worthwhile thought. These two prayers fill me with rapture and feed and satisfy my soul.

Reflection

There is a popular story from the life of St. John Vianney, the Curé of Ars, regarding a peasant from his parish. The peasant sat in church for a long time every day and Vianney asked him what he did as he sat there. "I look at him," the man answered, "and he looks at me, and we are happy together."

Thérèse would have approved of this man's simple, heartfelt approach to prayer. We may find prayer challenging, as she did, or serene, as the peasant did. The important thing is simply that we do pray, recognizing that prayer is not an end in itself but the opportunity for a personal encounter with God.

Prayer

Help me to be like Thérèse, Lord: faithful to prayer even when I'm tired or bored or feel that you don't hear me. As I reach out to you, reach out to me and draw me near through our mutual conversation. Through Christ our Lord. Amen.

SEVEN

The Church, Mary, and the Saints

THÉRÈSE WAS NOT a typical young nun. She was kind and devout and humble, of course, as were most of her fellow nuns. But Thérèse was also unconventional. She disliked retreats. She found prayer difficult. She had great trouble praying the rosary. She didn't care for spiritual reading, except for Scripture and a few other books. And in an age when frequent Communion was rare, she felt it should be encouraged.

Thérèse's love for the church, Mary, and the saints was marked by this strong thinking. Regarding frequent Communion, she didn't hesitate to point out that Jesus "does not come down from heaven every day to lie in a golden ciborium" but to rest in our hearts.

None of the sermons she heard about Mary impressed her in the least, especially those that presented Mary as a paragon of virtue, inaccessible to the ordinary person. She wished that she could have been a priest, she said, so that she could have preached about Mary as the holy but, in many ways, ordinary woman that she was.

As she lay dying, Thérèse kept near her bed various holy cards and pictures of the saints. She frequently appealed to the saints, and especially to the Blessed Virgin, in prayer. If they heard her, that was fine. If they didn't, she said, she loved them anyway. She never perceived them as exalted and unapproachable but as fellow travelers on the road of life who had gone before her.

In an age that tended to see religion as stern and unyielding, Thérèse spoke of God himself, his church, his mother, and the saints, with tremendous warmth and affection. The church was her home and these were her friends, her true family, those who accompanied her on the way home.

The Blessed in Heaven

I believe that the Blessed in heaven have a great compassion for our wretchedness. They remember that when they were frail and mortal like us they committed the same faults, endured the same struggles, and their fraternal love becomes greater even than it was on earth, which is why they do not cease to protect us and pray for us.

… [God] leads souls… by such different ways. When we read the lives of the saints, we find that many of them didn't trouble to leave anything behind them when they died, never a keepsake, never a scrap of writing.

Others, like our mother St. Teresa [of Avila], have enriched the treasury of the church with an account of the splendid revelations made to them. They weren't afraid of betraying these royal secrets of his, in the hope of making him better known and better loved.

Which kind does God like best? I don't think he has any preferences. All alike have been faithful to the guidance of his Holy Spirit.

When we pray to the Blessed Virgin and she does not hear us, we ought to let her do what she pleases without insisting, and not go on tormenting ourselves any further.

Thérèse recounted the following incident in a conversation with her sister Pauline. The communion of saints was a source of great consolation to Thérèse.

Sister Marie of the Eucharist wanted to light candles for a procession. She had no matches; however, seeing the little lamp that was burning in front of the relics, she approached it.

Alas, it was half out; there remained only a feeble glimmer on its blackened wick. She succeeded in lighting her candle from it, and with this candle, she lighted those of the whole community.

It was, therefore, the half-extinguished little lamp which had produced all these beautiful flames... nevertheless, it would always be the little lamp which would be first cause of all this light. How could the beautiful flames boast of having produced this fire, when they themselves were lighted with such a small spark?

It is the same with the communion of saints. Very often, without our knowing it, the graces and lights that we receive are due to a hidden soul, for God wills that the saints communicate grace to each other through prayer with great love, with a love much greater than that of a family, and even the most perfect family on earth.

How often have I thought that I may owe all the graces I've received to the prayers of a person who begged them from God for me, and whom I shall know only in heaven....

In heaven, we shall not meet with indifferent glances, because all the elect will discover that they owe to each other the graces that merited the crown for them.

Devotion to the Holy Eucharist

Thérèse longed to receive Communion every day but that was not the custom of the time. On some occasions, for various reasons, however, she received more often than usual.

[Jesus] gave himself to me in Holy Communion far oftener than I should have dared to hope. I had made it a rule to go very faithfully to every Communion allowed me by my confessor, but never to ask him to allow me more. In those days I hadn't the daring I have now, or I should have behaved quite differently, for I'm absolutely certain that people must tell their confessors of the longing they have to receive God.

For he does not come down from heaven every day to lie in a golden ciborium. He comes to find another heaven which is infinitely dearer to him—the heaven of our souls, created in his image, the living temples of the adorable Trinity!

Thérèse's cousin, Marie Guerin, was excessively concerned over imagined sins. This scrupulosity prevented her from receiving Communion.

She wrote to Thérèse. Thérèse, only sixteen years old, responded with a letter showing her astonishing grasp of the Eucharist. It was even more impressive since she wrote at a time when Communion was considered something of a rare privilege.

In 1910, when Thérèse's canonization was under consideration, this particular letter came to the attention of a priest working on Thérèse's cause. He brought it to Pope Pius X, who had written a decree urging Catholics to receive Communion more frequently. The priest pointed out that Thérèse had made an "anticipated" commentary on the Pope's decree.

... I think I must tell you something that has caused me great pain.... It is that my little Marie is not receiving Communion.... Oh! What pain that gives to Jesus!...

The devil must indeed be clever to deceive a soul like that!... But surely you know... that that is the one goal of his desires. He realises, treacherous creature that he is, that he cannot get a soul to sin if that soul wants to belong wholly to Jesus, so he only tries to make it think it is in sin.

It is already much for him to have put confusion into that soul, but his rage demands something more. He wants to deprive Jesus of a loved tabernacle. Since he cannot enter that sanctuary himself, he wants at least to have it remain empty and without [its] master!...

When the devil has succeeded in keeping a soul

away from Holy Communion, he has gained all.... Don't listen to the demon, laugh at him and go without fear to receive the Jesus of peace and love!...

[Thérèse] has also passed through the martyrdom of scruples, but Jesus gave her the grace to receive Communion all the same.... I assure you that she realises that it was the only way to get rid of the demon, for when he sees that he is wasting his time, he leaves you in peace.

No, it is not possible that a heart "that finds no rest save in the sight of the tabernacle" should offend Jesus enough to be unfit to receive him.... Receive Communion often, very often... there you have the sole remedy if you want to be cured....

Six weeks before her death, Thérèse had an insight into the importance of the Confiteor, the prayer of repentance said during the Mass.

... How great was this new grace which I received this morning at the moment when the priest began the Confiteor, before giving me Holy Communion!

I beheld our Lord all ready to give himself to me, and that confession appeared to me a very necessary humiliation: I confess to God, to Blessed Mary, ever virgin... and to all the saints... that I have sinned exceedingly.

"Oh yes," I said to myself, "one does well at this

moment to ask pardon for me from God and from all the saints." I felt myself to be, like the publican, a great sinner, and God appeared to me as being so merciful! I found that address to the whole heavenly court, to obtain through their intercession the forgiveness of my sins, to be so touching....

I had much difficulty in holding back my tears! And when the sacred host rested upon my lips I was strangely moved.... It was extraordinary to have had that experience at the Confiteor!

The Holy Family

Thérèse saw the Holy Family as down-to-earth and ordinary, as she illustrates here. She speaks out against the many apocryphal stories that for centuries were popular among Christians.

How charming it will be in heaven to know everything that took place in the Holy Family! When little Jesus began to grow up, perhaps when he saw the Blessed Virgin fasting, he said to her: "I would like to fast, too." And the Blessed Virgin answered: "No, little Jesus, you are still too little. You haven't got the strength." Or else perhaps she didn't dare hinder him from doing this.

And good St. Joseph! Oh! How I love him! He wasn't able to fast because of his work.

I can see him planing, then drying his forehead from time to time. Oh! How I pity him. It seems to me that their life was simple.

The country women came to speak familiarly with the Blessed Virgin. Sometimes they would ask her to entrust her little Jesus to them so that he would go and play with their children....

What does me a lot of good when I think of the Holy Family is to imagine a life that was very ordinary. It wasn't everything that they have told us or imagined. For example, that the child Jesus, after having formed some birds out of clay, breathed upon them and gave them life. Ah! No! Little Jesus didn't perform useless miracles like that, even to please his mother.

Why weren't they transported into Egypt which would have been necessary and so easy for God. In the twinkling of an eye, they could have been brought there. No, everything in their life was done just as in our own.

How many troubles, disappointments! How many times did others make complaints to good St. Joseph! How many times did they refuse to pay him for his work!

Oh! How astonished we would be if we only knew how much they had to suffer!

Mary and Her Maternal Love

Thérèse again takes up the theme of the ordinariness of Mary's life.

How very glad I should have been to be a priest, so as to preach about the Blessed Virgin!...

First, I should have shown how little is known of the life of the Blessed Virgin. It is not well to say things about her that are unlikely, or that we do not know for certain.... For example, that it was with feelings of extraordinary fervor and on fire with love that at the age of three she went to the temple to offer herself to God. Perhaps she went quite simply in obedience to her parents!

Again, regarding the prophetic words of the old man, Simeon, why insist that the Blessed Virgin from that moment had constantly before her eyes the passion of Jesus? "Thy own soul a sword shall pierce." You see very well... that it was a prediction of what was to come later on....

For a sermon on the Blessed Virgin to bear fruit it must manifest her real life, such as the Gospel has set it before us, and not her apocryphal life. We can well understand that her real life at Nazareth and the subsequent years must have been quite ordinary.... "He was subject to them." How simple that is!

Instead of showing the Blessed Virgin as all but inaccessible, we should hold her up as possible of imitation while practicing the hidden virtues, and living by faith just like us.

Thérèse stresses Mary's maternal love, knowing that it is easier to approach her as mother than under her more exalted title as Queen of Heaven.

We know very well that the Blessed Virgin is Queen of heaven and earth, but she is more mother than queen; and we should not say, on account of her prerogatives, that she surpasses all the saints in glory just as the sun at its rising makes the stars disappear from sight. My God! How strange that would be! A mother who makes her children's glory vanish! I myself think just the contrary. I believe she'll increase the splendor of the elect very much.

It's good to speak about her prerogatives, but we should not stop at this, and if, in a sermon, we are obliged from beginning to end to exclaim and say: Ah! Ah! We would grow tired!

Who knows whether some soul would not reach the point of feeling a certain estrangement from a creature so superior and would not say: If things are such, it's better to go and shine as well as one is able in some little corner!

What the Blessed Virgin has more than we have is the privilege of not being able to sin, she was exempt from the stain of original sin; but on the other hand, she wasn't as fortunate as we are, since she didn't have a Blessed Virgin to love. And this is one more sweetness for us and one less sweetness for her!

Thérèse insisted that Mary wanted not so much to be admired as to be imitated.

Let the priests, then, show us practicable virtues! It's good to speak of her privileges, but it's necessary above all that we can imitate her. She prefers imitation to admiration, and her life was so simple.... How I like singing to her: The narrow road to heaven you have made visible, when practicing always the most humble virtues.

Our Lady of Victories

When Thérèse was ten years old, she developed a mysterious illness that brought her close to death. Her symptoms included hallucinations and extreme fatigue. Thérèse said afterwards, "It was undoubtedly caused by the devil... who wished to punish me for the harm our family was to do him in the future."

When it seemed that there was no hope for Thérèse, her father wrote to the shrine of Our Lady of Victories in Paris and requested that a series of Masses be offered for Thérèse's recovery.

The Martins had a particular devotion to Our Lady of Victories and kept her statue in a place of honor. Mary had once spoken to Thérèse's mother as she prayed in front of it. That statue now stood beside Thérèse's bed.

On the Sunday, during the novena for me in Paris, Marie went into the garden and left me with Léonie. … After a minute or two I began calling, almost in a whisper: "Marie, Marie!"… Marie came in. I saw her quite clearly, but I did not recognize her and went on shouting…. Then, with Léonie and Céline, she knelt by my bed.

They gazed towards the statue of the Blessed Virgin and prayed to her with all the passion of a mother asking for the life of her child…. I could find no help on earth, so I also turned to my heavenly mother and beseeched her to have pity on me.

Suddenly the Blessed Virgin glowed with a beauty beyond anything I had ever seen. Her face was alive with kindness and an infinite tenderness, but it was an enchanting smile which really moved me to the depths. My pain vanished and two great tears crept down my cheeks—tears of pure joy.

I looked at Marie… [who] seemed moved as if

she guessed the favor granted me by the Blessed Virgin. It was indeed to her and to her prayers that I owed the grace of a smile from the queen of heaven. When she saw me staring at the statue, she said to herself: "Thérèse is cured!" She was right. The Little Flower had come back to life.

After Thérèse's miraculous healing, Marie goaded her into describing exactly what she had seen when Mary smiled. Thérèse had wanted to keep this secret, fearing that talking about it would diminish the incident.

In fact, Thérèse later recalled, the moment she told Marie what she had seen, "my happiness disappeared, and I bitterly regretted what I'd done. For four years the memory of that wonderful grace I'd received was a real torment to me, and when I found happiness again it was only at the feet of Our Lady of Victories."

She is referring to the pilgrimage the Martins took to Paris and Italy. While in Paris, Thérèse's father brought her to the Church of Our Lady of Victories and there Thérèse received confirmation that Mary had indeed brought about her healing from the mysterious illness.

Sight-seeing began as soon as we reached Paris. Dear Papa would spare no effort to amuse us, and it looked as if we should have worked through all the wonders of the capital in no time. There was only one of them that really took me out of myself, and that was Our Lady of Victories.

I can't describe what I felt, kneeling in front of the statue. I was so full of gratitude that it could only find its outlet (just as on my First Communion day) in tears. Our Lady gave me the assurance that she really had smiled at me, really had effected my cure.

I knew then that she really was watching over me, that I was her child. I began calling her "Mamma" because "Mother" didn't seem intimate enough.

Oh, I prayed so hard that she would go on looking after me, and would make my dream [of becoming a Carmelite] come true before long by taking me under the protection of her stainless robe. I'd wanted that from my earliest years and as I grew up I'd come to realise that, for me, Carmel was the only place where that shelter could be found.

The statue of Our Lady of Victories stood by Thérèse's bed during her childhood illness. Years later, it was placed by her bed as she lay dying in the infirmary.

The convent began a novena to Our Lady of Victories when it became apparent that Thérèse was seriously ill. The sisters were disappointed, but Thérèse herself never seemed to expect another miracle. However, she found great consolation in gazing at the statue and in praying to Mary. The following are some of Thérèse's comments pertaining to Mary spoken during the last days of her illness.

I'm perhaps losing my wits. Oh! If only they knew the weakness I'm experiencing. Last night, I couldn't take any more. I begged the Blessed Virgin to hold my head in her hands so that I could take my sufferings.

Pauline sat with Thérèse on the morning of the day of her death. Thérèse had had a difficult night and Pauline commented on the scene.

She was exhausted, gasping for breath; her sufferings, I thought, were indescribable. One moment she joined her hands and looked at the statue of the Blessed Virgin. "Oh! I prayed fervently to her," [Thérèse said]. "But it's the [death] agony, really, without any mixture of consolation."

Later, Thérèse said:
O my God!...
I love God!...
O good Blessed Virgin, come to my aid!...
If this is the agony, what is death?!...
[She looked at the statue of Mary and said]:
Oh! You know I'm suffocating!

When her sufferings reached a pitch, her mother prioress assured her that soon she'd be with "the Blessed Virgin and the child Jesus."

O Mother, present me quickly to the Blessed Virgin.
I'm a baby who can't stand any more. Prepare me
for death!

Pauline notes that at six o'clock, when the angelus
rang, Thérèse gazed at the statue for a long time.
Shortly after seven o'clock, she died.

Reflection

Like all the great saints, Thérèse belonged wholeheartedly to the church. She wasn't blind to its
problems and she had first-hand experience of the
shortcomings of its leaders. She had no false hopes,
no illusions, and no dangerous sentimentalism.

Thérèse was able to accept the good with the bad
because she knew that this was where she would best
meet Jesus. Everything she needed for the journey—
God himself, the Eucharist, the angels, Mary, the saints,
the sacraments—she found in the church.

Prayer

Lord, thank you for your mother. Help me to love
her and trust her as you did when you were on earth.

Thank you for the saints. They were sinners as we are sinners. They understand our weaknesses and are ready to intercede for us. Help me to draw close to them, to meet them as friends who will help me grow closer to you. Through Christ our Lord. Amen.

EIGHT

Giving Spiritual Direction: Reflecting Truth

Thérèse acted as the mistress of novices from the spring of 1893 until her strength gave out in 1897. She never officially bore the title but served as the assistant, first under her sister Pauline and then under Mother Marie de Gonzague. In practice, these women left the training of the young Carmelites to Thérèse who was herself only twenty when she took up the task.

If the novices expected to glide easily through their formation under the gentle, humble Thérèse, they had a rude awakening. She was tough and unrelenting in her determination to shape them.

"A soldier is not afraid of combat and I am a soldier," she said in reference to her struggles with one difficult novice. On her deathbed, Thérèse had to correct that same novice. "Didn't I tell you," she said, "that I would die with my weapons in my hand?"

Some of what Thérèse has to say about spiritual direction does not apply to lay people. She was training women for the religious life and worked within the structure of their vows. When she speaks of obedience, for example, she is often speaking of the very strict obedience to authority demanded by the vow of obedience.

On the other hand, much of what Thérèse offers is useful for anyone concerned with the spiritual development of others. Parents, especially, can adapt and apply much of Thérèse's advice to the formation of their children.

Thérèse excelled at her task and, in spite of her occasional severity, the novices loved her. Mother de Gonzague said that "[she] carried out the difficult charge of mistress of novices with a wisdom and perfection that was equalled only by her love for God."

She was able to do so with serenity because of her unwavering faith in the Lord. Thérèse didn't manipulate, plead, bargain, or berate. She simply did her best and then entrusted the particular novice or situation to the Lord.

"To the right and to the left, I throw to my little birds the good grain that God places in my hands. And then I let things take their course! I busy myself with it no more.... God tells me: 'Give, give always, without being concerned about the results.'"

Guiding Souls

Thérèse acknowledges that God is behind her success as director of the novices.

... I realised that I couldn't do anything by my own strength. I came to see that only one thing matters: Uniting myself more closely to the Lord all the time. Whatever else I want will be given me without the asking.

That's my experience—that my hopes haven't once been disappointed. Whenever my sisters were in need of spiritual food, God has seen fit to put it in my unworthy hands.

... If I had to depend in the slightest degree on my own strength, I should have handed in my papers long ago. When you look at it from a distance, it all seems plain sailing. What's the difficulty about doing good to souls, making them love God better—in a word, turning them out on your own pattern, according to your own ideas?

But when you look at it from close to, it's not plain sailing at all, nothing of the kind. You discover that trying to do good to people without God's help is no easier than making the sun shine at midnight.

You discover that you've got to abandon all your own preferences, your own bright ideas, and guide souls along the road our Lord has marked out for them. You mustn't dragoon them into some path of your own choosing.

The moment I began to deal with souls I realised instantly that the task was beyond my strength. I put myself quickly in the arms of God and behaved like babies who when frightened bury their heads on their father's shoulders.

I said: "Lord, you see that I am too little to feed your children. Put food into my hand if it is through me that you want to give each of them what is good for her. Without leaving your arms and without even turning my head, I will distribute your treasure to all the souls who come to ask me for food.

"When they like it, I shall know it is you they must thank, but if they complain that what I give them is bitter, I shall not be disturbed and shall try to persuade them that the food comes from you. And I shall take good care that it is all they get."

I learned a lot by teaching others. I discovered that every soul has almost the same difficulties and that there is yet a vast difference between individual souls—a difference which means that each one must be dealt with differently.

There are some with whom I must make myself small and show myself willing to be humiliated by confessing my own struggles and defeats, for then they themselves easily confess their own faults and are pleased that I understand them through my own experience.

To be successful with others, firmness is necessary. I must never go back on what I have said, and to humiliate myself would be regarded as weakness.

"The truth, the whole truth, and nothing but the truth." That's what Thérèse gave her novices. If they didn't want to hear it, she said, they ought to avoid her.

I was still very young when Aunt gave me a story to read that surprised me very much. I saw where they were praising a boarding school teacher because she was able to extricate herself cleverly from certain situations without offending anyone.

I took note above all of this statement: "She said to this one: You're not wrong; to that one, You are right." And I thought to myself: This is not good! This teacher should have had no fear and should have told her little girls that they were wrong when this was the truth.

And even now I haven't changed my opinion. I've had a lot of trouble over it, I admit, for it's always so easy to place the blame on the absent, and this immediately calms the one who is complaining.

Yes, but it is just the contrary with me. If I'm not loved, that's just too bad! I tell the whole truth, and if anyone doesn't wish to know the truth, let her not come looking for me.

Before I left the world, God gave me the consolation of contemplating at close range the souls of little children....

A poor woman, a relative of our maid, died when still very young and left three very little children. During the woman's illness, we took care of the two little girls. The older one was not yet six. I spent the whole day with them and it was a great pleasure for me to see with what simplicity they believed everything I said.

... I spoke to them about the eternal rewards that little Jesus would give in heaven to good little children. The older one, whose reasoning was beginning to develop, looked at me with eyes that were bright with joy, asking me a thousand charming questions about little Jesus and his beautiful heaven....

Seeing innocent souls at such close range, I understood what a misfortune it was when they were not formed in their early years, when they are soft as wax upon which one can imprint either virtue or vice.

I understood, too, what Jesus said: "But whoever causes one of these little ones to sin, it were better for him to have a great millstone fastened round his neck and to be drowned in the depths of the sea." Ah! How many souls would have reached sanctity had they been well directed!

Relying on God and Letting Go of Self-Interest

In a conversation with Pauline, Thérèse gives us a glimpse of how she relied on God to help her direct the novices. Sister Geneviève was her older sister, Céline, who, like all the novices, spent time privately with Thérèse.

When Sister Geneviève used to come to visit me, I wasn't able to say all I wanted to say in a half hour. Then, during the week, whenever I had a thought or else was sorry for having forgotten to tell her something, I would ask God to let her know and understand what I was thinking about, and in the next visit she'd speak to me exactly about the thing I had asked God to let her know.

At the beginning [of her time at Carmel], when she was really suffering and I was unable to console her, I would leave the visit with a heavy heart, but I soon understood it wasn't I who could console anyone; and then I was no longer troubled when she left very sad.

I begged God to supply for my weakness, and I felt he answered me. I would see this in the following visit. Since that time, whenever I involuntarily caused anyone any trouble, I would beg God to repair it, and then I no longer tormented myself with the matter.

Thérèse approached the spiritual direction of others with a complete lack of self-interest. She didn't care what the novices thought of her and she wasn't even concerned that her work bear fruit. She did her best and then left the situation in God's hands. This not only freed her from anxiety but forced each novice to take responsibility for her own development.

Ever since I took over the novitiate, my life has been one of war and struggle.... But the good God has done the work for me. I have labored for him and my soul has made astounding progress....

My only desire has been to please him. Consequently I have not worried over what others might be thinking or saying about me. I have not sought to be loved for myself, nor have I desired that my efforts bear fruit. True, we must sow the seed of goodness on all sides, but if it does not spring up, what matter! Our lot is to work, the victory is for Jesus.

When there is question of doing good to our neighbor, we must let nothing deter us nor pass over anything to make things easier for ourselves. As for reprimands, our intention in giving them must be directed first to the glory of God and must not spring from a desire to succeed in enlightening the novices.

Moreover, in order that a correction bear fruit, it must cost in the giving, and the heart must be free from the least shadow of passion.

Correction

Thérèse's advice on correction can easily be applied to the home front. Parents need to discipline their children with love but also with courage, not falling prey to guilt or sentimentalism.

We should never allow kindness to degenerate into weakness. When we have scolded someone with just reason, we must leave the matter there, without allowing ourselves to be touched to the point of tormenting ourselves for having caused pain or at seeing one suffer and cry.

To run after the afflicted one to console her does more harm than good. Leaving her to herself forces her to have recourse to God in order to see her faults and humble herself.

Otherwise, accustomed to receiving consolation after a merited reprimand, she will always act, in the same circumstances, like a spoiled child, stamping her feet and crying until her mother comes to dry her tears.

Reflection

Giving and receiving direction is a touchy business. Both parties may fall victim to pride, one convinced that the advice is helpful, the other convinced that the director is not sensitive to his or her needs. In fact, both may be completely wrong.

Terrible damage has been done not only through misguided spiritual direction but also through the stubborn refusal to accept good advice. Thérèse skirted these hazards by leaving each situation to the Lord and not insisting on her own way. She stayed close to God, gave the direction she thought best, and left the consequences to the Lord.

Prayer

Lord, help me to welcome into my life all those people whose advice and insight can lead me closer to you. Sometimes what they have to say may be painful and I won't want to hear it. Help me to overcome my resistance so that I can be all that you've called me to be. Through Christ our Lord. Amen.

NINE

Zeal, Intercessory Prayer, and Conversion

No SAINT SEEMS A LESS LIKELY CANDIDATE for patron saint of the missions than Thérèse of Lisieux. Yet she shares that honor with St. Francis Xavier, a widely traveled and more logical choice. Francis, it is said, converted hundreds of thousands and endured harrowing conditions during his travels through the east.

Thérèse, on the other hand, never left her cloister for the nine years of her religious life, apparently converted no one, wrote no treatises on evangelization, never preached to large crowds, never baptized anyone, and never engaged in fundraising. To all apearances, she did nothing more than pursue her "little way" among the twenty-five or so nuns of her own convent.

But the church recognizes in Thérèse a most unusual and intense missionary spirit: She proposes to "spend her heaven doing good on earth," bringing souls to Jesus. "If my wishes are granted," she said, "my heaven will be spent on earth until the end of the world."

Not even Francis, the consummate missionary, makes such an extravagant claim. Earthbound, he accomplished miraculous conversions. Thérèse couldn't compete with him in life, but she has matched him in death. Shortly after she died, accounts of restored relationships, conversions, and healings granted through her intercession began to pour into the Carmel of Lisieux.

The foundation for Thérèse's heavenly activity, however, was the zeal for souls that gripped her on earth. She was consumed with a thirst for souls, she said. Her life was nothing less than an apostolate of prayer and suffering for sinners. Even on her deathbed, in the midst of terrible pain, she insisted that the prayers offered for her relief be offered, instead, on behalf of sinners.

Thérèse's zeal sprang from her love for God and his love for her. This was too good to keep to herself. The point of her life, she said, was to love Jesus wholeheartedly "and to save souls so that he may be loved by them."

A Fisher of Souls

Even before Thérèse entered the convent, she was convinced that Jesus had made her "a fisher of souls." "I experienced a great desire to work for the conversion of sinners," she said. She had her first success in this line when she prayed for the salvation of an unrepentant murderer named Pranzini. The event was crucial in launching Thérèse on her apostolate of prayer. Céline offered to join her in interceding for the man.

I would have liked all creation to join with me in praying for the grace that was needed [by Pranzini]. In my heart I felt certain we shouldn't be disappointed, but by way of encouragement in this practice of praying for sinners, I did ask for a sign.... I would like him to show some sign of repentance, just for my own satisfaction.

My prayer was answered and to the letter.... The day after his execution I came upon a copy of *La Croix* [a newspaper]. I lost no time in opening it, and what I read brought the tears to my eyes....

Pranzini didn't go to confession. He went up on to the scaffold, and was just preparing to put his head through the bars of the guillotine, when a sudden inspiration came to him. He availed himself of the crucifix which the priest was holding out to him and kissed, three times, the sacred wounds. And with that, his soul went to receive its award from those merciful lips which told us that "there will be more rejoicing in heaven over one sinner who repents than over ninety-nine souls that are justified and have no need of repentance...."

After that special grace, my longing to save souls grew from day to day.... I offered to our Lord souls that were revivified, now, by the dew of his precious blood. And the more I did that, the more he, on his side, increased in my imperfect nature the thirst for souls....

One Sunday, looking at a picture of our Lord on the cross, I was struck by the blood flowing from one of the divine hands. I felt a great pang of sorrow when thinking this blood was falling to the ground without anyone's hastening to gather it up.

I was resolved to remain in spirit at the foot of the cross and to receive the divine dew. I understood I was then to pour it out upon souls.

The cry of Jesus on the cross sounded continually in my heart: "I thirst!" These words ignited within me an unknown and very living fire. I wanted to give my beloved to drink and I felt myself consumed with a thirst for souls.... I burned with the desire to snatch [great sinners] from the eternal flames.

Thérèse was asked to correspond with a missionary priest who requested the prayers and support of one of the nuns of Carmel. She wrote to him concerning her zeal for souls.

... I don't want you to ask God to deliver me from the flames of purgatory. St. Teresa [of Avila] said to her daughters, when they wanted to pray for themselves: "What care I if I stay in purgatory till the end of the world, if I save a single soul by my prayers."

That phrase finds an echo in my heart. I want to save souls and forget self for them. I want to save them even after my death so I should be happy if... you would say: "My God, permit my sister to go on making you loved."

When I was beginning to learn the history of France, the account of Joan of Arc's exploits delighted me. I felt in my heart the desire and the courage to imitate her. It seemed the Lord destined me, too, for great things.

I was not mistaken, but instead of voices from heaven inviting me to combat, I heard in the depths of my soul a gentler and stronger voice, that of the spouse of virgins, who was calling me to other exploits, to more glorious conquests and into Carmel's solitude.

I understood my mission was not to have a mortal king crowned but to make the king of heaven loved, to submit to him the kingdom of hearts.

... One day when I was thinking of what I could do to save souls, a word of the Gospel gave me a real light. In days gone by, Jesus said to his disciples when showing them the fields of ripe corn: "Lift up your eyes and see how the fields are already white enough to be harvested," and a little later: "In truth, the harvest is abundant but the number of laborers is small. Ask then the master of the harvest to send laborers."

What a mystery! Is not Jesus all powerful? Are

not creatures his who made them? Why, then, does Jesus say: "Ask the Lord of the harvest that he send some workers"? Why?

Ah, it is because Jesus has so incomprehensible a love for us that he wills that we have a share with him in the salvation of souls. He wills to do nothing without us. The Creator of the universe awaits the prayer of a poor little soul to save other souls redeemed like it at the price of all his blood.

I hold nothing in my hands. Everything I have, everything I merit, is for the church and for souls.

If I had been rich, I would have found it impossible to see a poor person going hungry without giving him my possessions.

And in the same way, when I gain any spiritual treasures, feeling that at this very moment there are souls in danger of being lost and falling into hell, I give them what I possess, and I have not yet found a moment when I can say: "Now I'm going to work for myself."

Praying for Priests

At the direction of St. Teresa of Avila, the sixteenth-century reformer of the Carmelite Order, the Carmelites have made a specific commitment to pray for priests.

When Thérèse entered the order she said that she had come "to save souls and especially to pray for priests." The next few selections indicate how seriously she took that commitment.

… Let us pray for priests. Each day shows how rare are the friends of Jesus. It seems to me that that is what he must feel most… ingratitude, especially when he sees souls consecrated to him giving to others the heart which belongs to him in so absolute a fashion.

On her trip to Rome, Thérèse gained insight into the importance of praying for priests.

… Another discovery I made concerned priests. Until then I hadn't been able to understand the main purpose of Carmel. I loved praying for sinners, but I was astounded at having to pray for priests. I thought their souls were without blemish.

It was in Italy that I came to understand my vocation, and I didn't have too far to travel to learn that. I met many holy priests during the month I was away, but I saw that some of them were still men, weak and subject to human frailty, even though the sublime dignity of the priesthood raised them above the angels.

Now if prayers are needed for those holy priests whom Jesus called "the salt of the earth," how much more is needed for priests of lukewarm virtue. For did not Jesus also ask: "If salt loses its taste, what is there left to give taste to?"

What a wonderful vocation we Carmelites have! It is up to us to preserve the salt of the earth. We offer our prayers and penance for God's apostles and we are their apostles while, by word and deed, they bring the gospel to our brethren.

In two letters to Céline, Thérèse conveys a sense of urgency in the matter of praying for priests.

Céline, during the brief moments that remain to us, let us not waste our time. Let us save souls. Souls "are lost like snowflakes" and Jesus weeps.... Let us live for souls, let us be apostles, especially let us save the souls of priests, souls which should be more transparent than crystal.

Alas, how many bad priests there are, how many who are not holy enough! Let us pray, let us suffer for them, and on the last day Jesus will be grateful. We shall give him souls.

Céline, I feel that Jesus is asking us... to slake his thirst by giving him souls, souls of priests above all.... We are so small a matter yet Jesus wills that the salvation of souls should depend on our sacrifices, our love. He is a beggar begging us for souls.

Spending Heaven Doing Good on Earth

The next excerpts document Thérèse's determination to continue her work for the church after her death.

I am perfectly sure I shall not stay inactive in heaven. My desire is to go on working for the church and for souls. That is what I keep asking God and I am certain he will say yes.

After all, the angels are continually occupied with us, while yet they never cease to see the face of God, and are rapt forever in the shoreless ocean of his love. Why should not Jesus permit me to do as they do?

How unhappy I should be in heaven if I could not provide little pleasures for those I love on earth.

I feel my mission is about to begin, my mission of making souls love the good God as I love him, to teach my little way to souls. If my desires receive fulfillment, I shall spend my heaven on earth even until the end of time.

Yes, I will spend my heaven doing good upon earth. That is not impossible, since from the midst of the beatific vision itself the angels watch over us.

No. I shall not be able to take my rest until the end of the world, as long as there are souls to be saved. But when the angel shall declare, "Time shall be no longer," then shall I take my rest, because the number of the elect will be complete, and all souls shall have entered into their joy and their rest.

I cannot dwell long on the thought of the happiness awaiting me in heaven. One expectation alone makes my heart beat fast: It is the love I shall receive and the love I shall be able to give.

I am thinking about all the wonderful things I should like to do after my death: to baptize little children, to aid priests and missionaries, and to assist the entire church.

Reflection

There was no conflict in Thérèse's mind between her intense desire to save souls and the cloistered life, where she was cut off from those souls. She knew she didn't need to be on the spot in order to bring an individual to the Lord.

All Thérèse's missionary work, all her "evangelism," took place through prayer and sacrifice. "Prayer is my greatest weapon," she once said and she wielded it effectively.

Thérèse gets us back to the basics of evangelism:

not techniques, books, or programs but prayer, sacrifice, and a heart set on God.

Prayer

Lord, give me a zealous heart. Renew in me the desire to bring others to you. When I do bring your word to those who don't know you, keep me humble and close to you. May your own compassion fill and guide me. Through Christ our Lord. Amen.

APPENDIX ONE

Answered Prayer

IT SEEMS THAT Thérèse's wish has come true: She has spent her heaven doing good on earth. Some of the most moving accounts of her assistance come from the battlefields of World War I. Thérèse had not yet been beatified, a preliminary step toward canonization, but many soldiers read her autobiography and adopted her as a kind of patron saint.

In the interest of hastening her canonization and out of simple gratitude for her protection, many of these men sent their stories of Thérèse's intervention to the Carmel at Lisieux.

Answered Prayer During World War I

The following letter was written by a French soldier, Paul-Henri Joly. The religious brother whom Joly mentions also wrote to Lisieux, attesting to Joly's character and strong faith.

Among all the dangers I met with, I must note in particular the battle of July 30th and of the following days. We were then on the Somme and ordered to go and reinforce the troops of the first line.

I served as communicating agent and we had to undergo the most terrible bombardments for four whole days....

One evening, the second of August, we were, a half section of us, crouched around the ruins of a house that was being blown to atoms under a hail of shrapnel. A religious, who was one of the group, exhorted us to pray under this ever-increasing danger, and my comrades recited the rosary.

As for me, while praying to the Blessed Virgin, I invoked Sister Thérèse, calling her confidently to our help. Suddenly, about eleven o'clock, while the battle raged, I saw her standing at the foot of one of the guns. She looked at me and blessed us all. Then she said to me, smiling, "Fear not, I come here to protect you."

Quite excited, I cried out to my companions: "I see Sister Thérèse, she is there! We are saved!" And in fact, not one of us fell, and we soon returned safe and sound from this awful position.

Another soldier recounted how Thérèse brought him back to health, mentally and spiritually.

I owe my dear little Sister Thérèse a great debt of gratitude for having directed me into the right path. Feeling myself cut off by my great sins, I was separating myself from God. The terrible experiences of the war had shattered my nervous system. Weariness and depression had settled upon me.

It was in such a condition that one night I entered, more or less mechanically, one of our churches which had not been entirely demolished by the enemy's shells. On coming away, I saw a few pamphlets scattered about, one of which I took with me–it was a life of Sister Thérèse of the Child Jesus. From the very first lines I was deeply moved and found myself, on finishing, a new man.

My mind was firmly made up to follow in the footsteps and act up to the principles of this saint for before such purity I could not remain cold or indifferent.

Since that time, when in the front-line trenches, I have ever placed the greatest trust in our dear little sister. Lightheartedness has returned to me and my energy has increased ten-fold. She has, over and over again, given me the courage to volunteer my services for perilous missions, and she has heard all my prayers.

But Sister Thérèse's intervention was most marked at the beginning of 1917. I was preserved from death in a position where escape was possible only through a miracle. I have since been saved from every danger, exempt from even the slightest wound. I carry a relic of her… and in order to do her honor, I will remain a brave and conscientious Christian to the end of my life.

Father L. Duflot was devoted to Thérèse and offered a Mass at least once a week for her beatification. On December 18, 1917, his church at Bethune was destroyed during a bombing raid. He was in the church at the time and though several people near him were killed during the attack, he was spared.

… On the morning of December 18… while at the altar, I was seized with inexpressible anguish at the moment of the Offertory. Then I turned towards the Sacred Heart and murmured: "What do you wish me to understand by this, O Lord?" And it seemed to me that I received this answer from within: "Be not fearful, I will deliver you."

In the evening, at half past four, I again experienced before the tabernacle, this very same extraordinary and undefinable sadness. At five o'clock, before giving Benediction of the Most Holy Sacrament, I came out of the sacristy preceded by the choir boys and followed by the organist and the chanter when, scarcely had I advanced a step along our narrow passage, then a frightful explosion thundered behind me.

Awe-stricken and deafened, contracting my shoulders beneath an avalanche of stones, I became, for a moment, unconscious. But suddenly, under the influence, it may be, of a violent and sudden current of air, I regained consciousness and rose up.

I then perceived, arriving herself ahead of this column of air, the little Sister Thérèse. Her scapular was waving in the wind and she appeared to be carried along. Stopping in front of me, she looked on me compassionately and addressed me with the one word: "Depart!"

I obeyed on the moment... although I was losing much blood through a wound in my head and in my leg....

Old professor of philosophy that I am, and endowed with an unemotional temperament, I don't think there is anything of the visionary about me. I possess, then, the deep conviction that I saw, with my own two eyes, the features of my loving protectress, in the midst of that mournful scene....

Sergeant Marcel Dutoit, wounded on the battlefield, expected to be taken as a prisoner of war. Instead, he was rescued by some French peasants who hid him on their farm.

... Scarcely had they concealed me in their barn, in company with two horses, when the German soldiers entered the farm and explored it on all sides to find me, but it was in vain and they withdrew crestfallen.

I lived thus a week with these good peasants and in spite of searches made as many as ten times a day to find me, never had any of the enemy come into the place where I was hiding. I was clearly convinced that Sister Thérèse preserved me and I have not failed to invoke her at every new attempt. I seemed even to see her before the door forbidding an entrance.

On one occasion, among others, my kind hosts

came in all haste to tell me: "It's all up! The Germans are here." Then I begged my powerful protectress to get me out of this last danger and I saw all at once these words written in white letters above the door: "Be not afraid. You will be saved."

In fact, the soldiers visited the neighboring barns and the yards without coming to look for me. Finally, thanks to the dear saint, I was picked up after eight days by an English patrol.

Many devout officers placed their regiments under the protection of Thérèse. Father Fromont, an army chaplain, described the circumstances that led one lieutenant to dedicate his troops to her.

… We were massed behind the Marne with our guns, horses and wagons. We had to cross the river but the Germans began to fire on the only bridge of Mézy.

Lieutenant L., who commands the seventeenth battery of this section of the artillery, was at a loss to know what to do. It was impossible to move to the right and the Germans were on our left. The only way open was the bridge, riddled by the bombardment.

In this extremity, he vowed to dedicate his battery to Sister Thérèse and dashed forward. From that moment, not a single shell hit the bridge and, wonder of wonders, the Germans stopped firing.

The lieutenant intends to keep his promise and I shall say the Mass, the day he will dedicate his battery to Sister Thérèse.

This soldier didn't ask for Thérèse's help, but she gave it anyway.

In my village I often heard of Sister Thérèse but without acquiring any particular devotion to her. In spite of this, she came to my assistance unasked. Here is how it happened.

After being called up, I was sent from battlefield to battlefield across the whole front. At first, I accepted the cross of the war as a heaven-sent chastisement. France, as a nation, had offended God so much that it seemed to me to be no more than our due.

But the long continued physical and moral sufferings wore down my courage and confidence and... I began to complain.... In this frame of mind, I arrived at Verdun....

Bivouacked in a ruined house, and having for bed some half rotten straw, I was spreading my blanket over it when my hand encountered some hard object.... I drew out a rather large volume which I placed under my head [as a pillow].

In the morning I opened the book. It was *The Story of a Soul*.... I began to read it and I found it so redolent of the love of God, and of holy submission to his will, that I was ashamed of my own weakness.

Hitherto, I had distrusted the Divine Goodness... but now I took a resolution to amend, relying on the little Sister, who had pointed out to me the right path....

Soldiers pinned Thérèse's picture to the dirt walls of trenches, carried her relics in their knapsacks, and wore her medal on their uniforms. R. Courdent, a Lazarist Missionary, reported the following amusing incident, indicating how wide-spread devotion to Thérèse had become.

A military chaplain, when on his way to the outposts, was caught in a shower of shells. Throwing himself on the ground, he crawled to a place of shelter hard-by, where he met a superior officer, a major.

After some minutes the latter, noticing the priest's coolness, said to him: "I bet you, Father, that you have the relic of little Sister Thérèse about you. If you haven't, your courage is inexplicable to me. As for myself, it has been my shield during thirty-two months service."

The chaplain in question was Father Delattre, the Assumptionist, who was awarded the Cross of the Legion of Honor....

Answered Prayer Today

Thérèse's intervention didn't end with the conclusion of World War I. She continues to send a "shower of roses," as she had promised, to those who seek her intercession.

The following stories are from Anne, a woman from the midwest whose grandmother passed on her great devotion to St. Thérèse. "When I first got close to Thérèse, I was in my early twenties, about her age toward the end of her life," Anne said. "She became like a friend to me."

While she frequently asks for Thérèse's intercession, Anne doesn't often ask for a sign—"only if I really need it," she said. On at least two occasions, she received answers to her prayers that exceeded her expectations.

In 1975 my husband, Joe, received a wonderful job offer. Unfortunately, the job required a move to another city and we were concerned about the impact that would have on our four children. Also, my husband and I had grown up in the area we lived in and we had a tremendous network of family and friends.

Still, the job would have brought Joe a lot more money and opportunity and we had a difficult time making the decision. We debated it endlessly until one night, in desperation, I prayed privately to the Little Flower and asked for a sign indicating whether we should stay where we were.

The next day, I decided to clean out a storage closet in a bedroom over the garage. We didn't use the closet very often but when I opened the door, I found fresh rose petals scattered over the closet floor. I was so shocked I ran and got a neighbor to come see.

That was the sign we needed and we turned down the job. Our decision proved to be an even bigger blessing than we expected because seven years later, Joe began to develop symptoms of Alzeheimers disease and nine years later, he died. Had we moved away, we would have been without the support of family and friends and would have had to move back home, disrupting our family all over again.

In 1993, Anne and Joe's thirty year old son, David, was arrested on drug charges. He was released on bond and over the next two years, his case made its way to trial. "The family was in unbelievable turmoil over this," Ann said. "Some days I didn't think I could put one foot in front of the other."

Finally, David appeared before the judge who sentenced him to seven to ten years in prison. The judge had the option to call him back after 90 days in prison and release him on probation or order him to complete his sentence.

"As those 90 days passed," Anne said, "we were all feeling tremendous anxiety. I was so distraught that I prayed and asked St. Thérèse to give me a sign so that I could calm down and pray and work fruitfully.

"That same day, I took a walk in a field where I often walked and prayed. As I approached the lake in this field, I saw a wild rose bush covered with red roses. I had never seen a single rose on this bush before and I had seen this bush almost every day in every season. I was jubilant and realized it was my sign.

"The judge did call our son back and released him. Since then, David has pulled his life together, has a job and has developed a life of very deep faith."

A priest from Colorado had an experience of Thérèse's intervention when he had some questions regarding prayer and fasting.

The Carmelite saints such as Teresa of Avila, John of the Cross and Thérèse of Lisieux all speak of the need for prayer, fasting and penance for those who want to grow in the spiritual life. During the summer of 1991, I began to practice fasting and penance more seriously and found that it made me more aware of and sensitive to sin and injustice.

Nevertheless, towards the end of the summer I began to ask myself if these practices were really as valuable as I thought. I had a long talk with a Carmelite priest who lives a penitential life and has been a good priestly model for me. Although he fasts and does penance, he pointed out that you have to remain prudent about such things in order to stay centered on Jesus and avoid pride.

I went to St. Thérèse with my question: Should I continue to integrate fasting and penance into my life? I asked her to send me one rose if I should give these things up. If I were to continue, I asked her to send me two or more roses. I told no one but my Carmelite friend about this petition.

Four days later I celebrated a home Mass for a woman and three of her close friends. As I was getting ready to go, one of them handed me a vase with forty-eight roses in it! I was shocked and surprised.

She said: "Our Lady wanted you to have these but we didn't know why." I said it was an answer to prayer.

Since then, I've read a lot about the value of fasting and penance. It strengthens the spirit, purifies the soul and helps one to resist temptation and sin. I will continue to fast and do penance and encourage others to do the same.

Timeline of Thérèse's Life

January 2, 1873	Thérèse Martin is born in Alençon, France.
August 28, 1877	Zélie Martin dies.
August 29, 1877	Thérèse asks Pauline to be her mother.
November 1877	The Martins move to Lisieux to be near their cousins.
October 2, 1882	Pauline enters Carmel at Lisieux.
October 3, 1882	Thérèse begins school at the Benedictine Abbey in Lisieux.
March–May 1883	She is seriously ill.
May 13, 1883 (*Pentecost*)	She is cured after seeing a statue of the Blessed Virgin smile.
May 8, 1884	She receives her First Communion.
May 22, 1884	She receives the holy desire to suffer.
June 14, 1884	She receives the Sacrament of Confirmation and with it the strength to suffer.

October 15, 1886	Marie enters Lisieux Carmel.
December 25, 1886	Thérèse's "Christmas conversion." She is freed from hypersensitivity and receives the desire to save souls.
May 1, 1887	Louis Martin suffers small stroke.
May 29, 1887 *(Pentecost)*	Louis gives Thérèse permission to enter the Carmelite Order.
July 13, 1887	Thérèse begins to pray for the conversion of the murderer, Pranzini.
September 1, 1887	She learns of Pranzini's confession before his execution.
November 20, 1887	She appeals to the pope to allow her to enter Carmel.
April 9, 1888	She enters the Carmel at Lisieux.
June 1888	Further decline of Louis Martin; he flees to Le Havre.
January 10, 1889	She receives the habit.
February 12, 1889	Louis Martin placed in Bon Sauveur Hospital.
September 8, 1890	Thérèse makes her profession.
September 24, 1890	She receives the veil.
May 12, 1892	Louis Martin makes final visit to the Lisieux Carmel.
February 20, 1893	Pauline elected to a term as prioress; asks Thérèse to help in the formation of novices.
July 29, 1894	Louis Martin dies.

September 14, 1894	Céline enters the Lisieux Carmel.
December 1894	Pauline asks Thérèse to write down memories of her childhood.
June 11, 1895	Thérèse offers herself as a victim of Merciful Love; Céline joins her in this offering.
August 15, 1895	Marie Guerin, the Martins' cousin, enters the Lisieux Carmel.
March 21, 1896	Marie de Gonzague again elected prioress.
April 2, 1896	Thérèse coughs up blood.
April 3, 1896	She again coughs up blood.
April 5, 1896 (*Easter Sunday*)	She enters into her trial of faith.
September 13–16, 1896	Thérèse writes reflections on love and her little way for her sister, Marie. It will be added to Thérèse's autobiography.
April, 1897	She becomes seriously ill.
June 3, 1897	She continues her autobiography at the request of Mother Marie.
August 19, 1897	She receives Communion for the last time.
September 30, 1897	Thérèse dies at about 7:20 in the evening.
September 30, 1898	Two thousand copies of *The Story of a Soul* are printed.

June 10, 1914	Pope Pius X signs the decree for the introduction of Thérèse's cause for canonization.
April 29, 1923	Thérèse beatified.
May 17, 1925	Thérèse canonized.